SPECTACULAR ANIMALS

Modern Publishing
A Division of Unisystems, Inc.
New York, New York 10022

CONTENTS

INTRODUCTION

Did you know that when a baby blue whale is born it weighs five times as much as your family automobile, and after it grows up it is the biggest animal that has ever lived? Did you know that the biggest land animals in the Antarctic are insects? That poisonous snakes can live up to a year without eating? Or that sharks have lived on the Earth for 350 million years, which makes them even older than dinosaurs? These are just a few of the amazing facts you will learn from *Spectacular Animals.*

Learn all about whales and dolphins, kangaroos and other marsupials, polar animals, crocodiles and alligators, and poisonous snakes—where they live, what they look like, what they eat and how they survive. It is filled with full-color photographs and drawings that will enhance your understanding of these animals and their daily lives. Chapters conclude with an Identification Chart to help you recognize the animals when you see them in the wild or in zoos and wildlife parks, and a game or activity that uses what you have learned about them. Each page highlights some of the surprising facts that make these animals truly spectacular. In addition, each chapter contains a Survival File that lets you know which animals are endangered species, and why.

The animals in this book have lived successfully on the Earth for hundreds of thousands, some of them even millions of years by adapting themselves to the requirements of their own environments, and they continue to adapt today.

Prepare for a wonderful journey as you begin an excursion into the spectacular World of Wildlife.

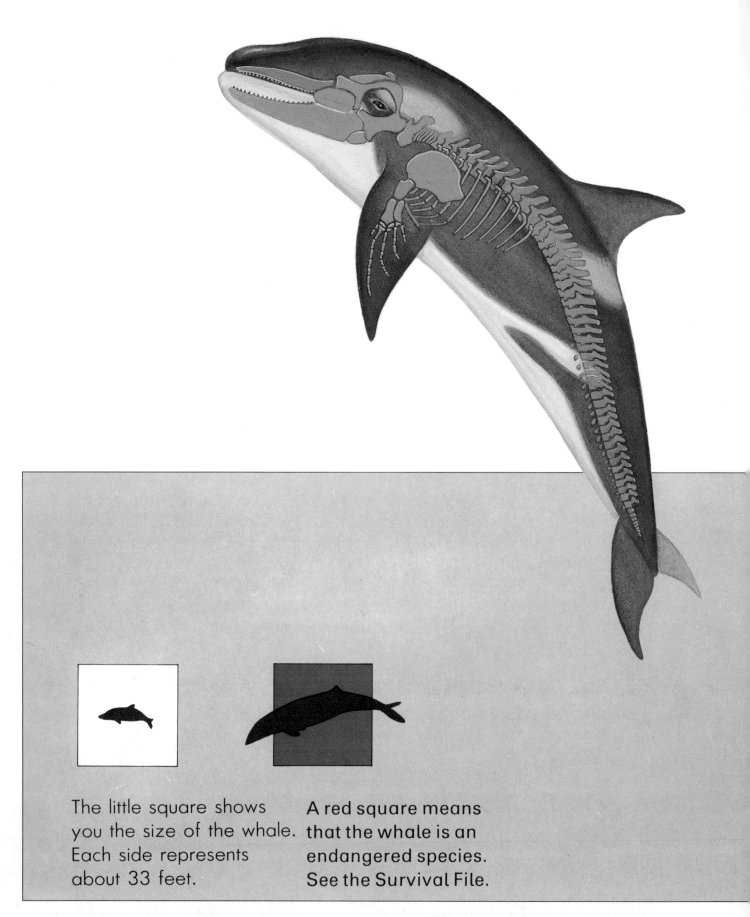

The little square shows you the size of the whale. Each side represents about 33 feet.

A red square means that the whale is an endangered species. See the Survival File.

A Humpback Whale leaps clear of the water ▷

Chapter 1
WHALES
AND
DOLPHINS

Lionel Bender

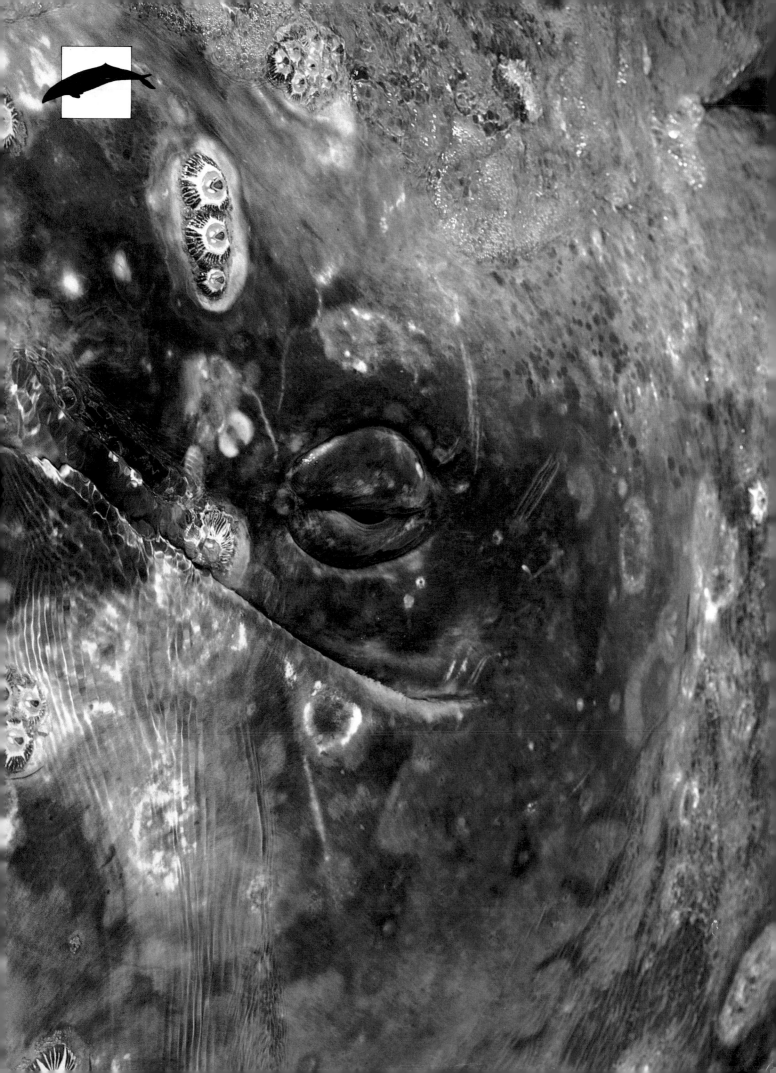

Facts to Know

The whales include the biggest animals ever known to exist. They also include the fastest swimmers alive. Some, like the Sperm Whale, descend to the ocean depths and are easily the deepest divers among the mammals. The small whales, the dolphins, are some of the most intelligent and playful of animals.

Whales enjoy being in groups and many are friendly towards people. But several kinds of whales have been hunted, by people, almost to extinction.

Because they live completely at sea, little is known about the life of many whales. This book tells just some of the fascinating and surprising things known about these animals. Much more is still to be learned.

The picture opposite shows the head of a Gray Whale

Seagoing mammals

Although whales and dolphins resemble fish, they are in fact mammals like us. They are warm-blooded, they breathe air using lungs, and they give birth to live babies, which feed on their mother's milk. Whales had ancestors that lived on land as most mammals do. But for the last 50 million years they have lived in the sea.

Like fish, whales are streamlined for swimming. But a whale swims by up-and-down movements of its tail, not side-to-side movements like a fish. Its front limbs are flippers, not fins. These have the same pattern of bones as we have in our arms and hands. The back limbs have disappeared over time. A whale's skin is smooth and has a few hairs, while a fish has a scaly skin.

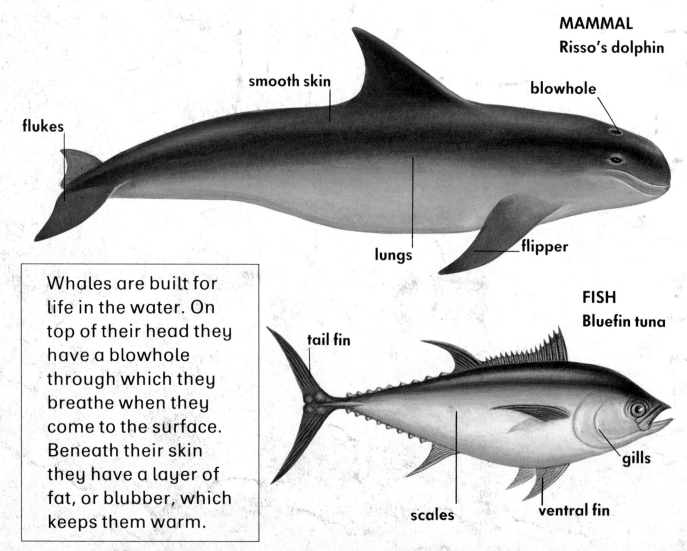

MAMMAL
Risso's dolphin

smooth skin

blowhole

flukes

lungs

flipper

Whales are built for life in the water. On top of their head they have a blowhole through which they breathe when they come to the surface. Beneath their skin they have a layer of fat, or blubber, which keeps them warm.

FISH
Bluefin tuna

tail fin

gills

scales

ventral fin

Although 50 feet long, the Humpback Whale glides easily through the ▷ **water**

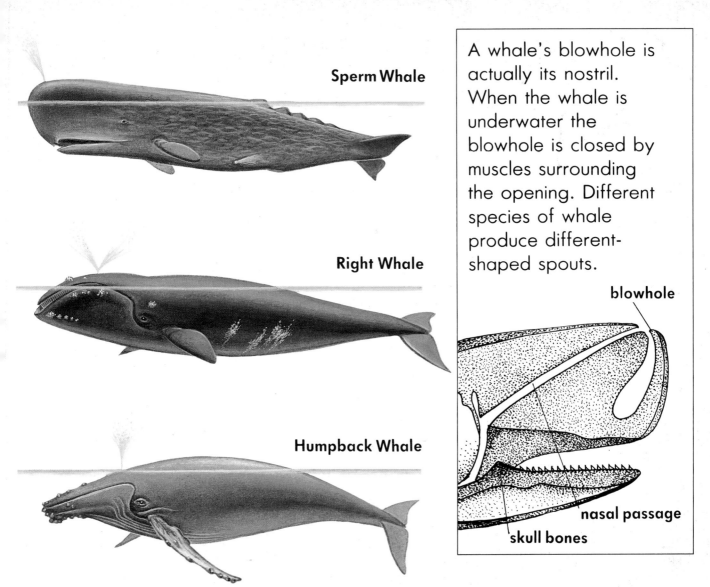

Sperm Whale

Right Whale

Humpback Whale

A whale's blowhole is actually its nostril. When the whale is underwater the blowhole is closed by muscles surrounding the opening. Different species of whale produce different-shaped spouts.

blowhole

nasal passage

skull bones

Breathing

Many whales can dive to great depths. A Sperm Whale can go down to more than 1.8 miles and stay underwater for 1¹/₂ hours at a time. Yet a whale must come to the surface to breathe. When it resurfaces, it pushes out used air through its blowhole, creating the familiar spout. It then takes a series of deep breaths before diving again.

In proportion to its body size, a whale's lungs are actually smaller than ours. But it fills its lungs much more fully than we do. A whale changes about 90 percent of the air in its lungs at each breath, while we change only about 12 percent. It also carries a store of oxygen in its muscles.

◁ **The Blue Whale blows an upright spout up to 33 feet high**

Moving

Even huge species like the 50-foot long Humpback Whale are natural acrobats and extremely agile swimmers. When they come up from a dive they may launch themselves completely out of the water and twist around in the air before crashing back through the surface. Dolphins often swim in groups in front of ships at sea, riding the bow waves like surfers.

Whales push themselves through the water by beating their tail flukes up and down with powerful body muscles. They use their flippers for steering. The water rushes easily over their smooth, oily skin. They can change the shape of their body surface to cope with the huge water pressure deep in the sea.

Diving Humpback Whale

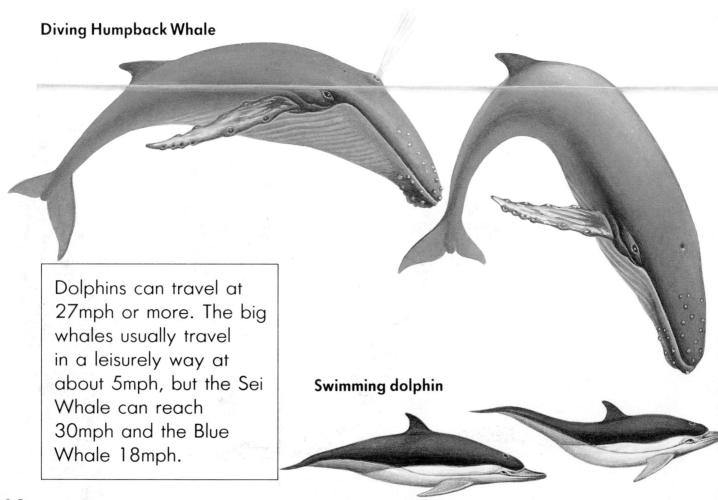

Swimming dolphin

Dolphins can travel at 27mph or more. The big whales usually travel in a leisurely way at about 5mph, but the Sei Whale can reach 30mph and the Blue Whale 18mph.

△ **The Blue Whale's tail flukes are seen briefly as it dives**

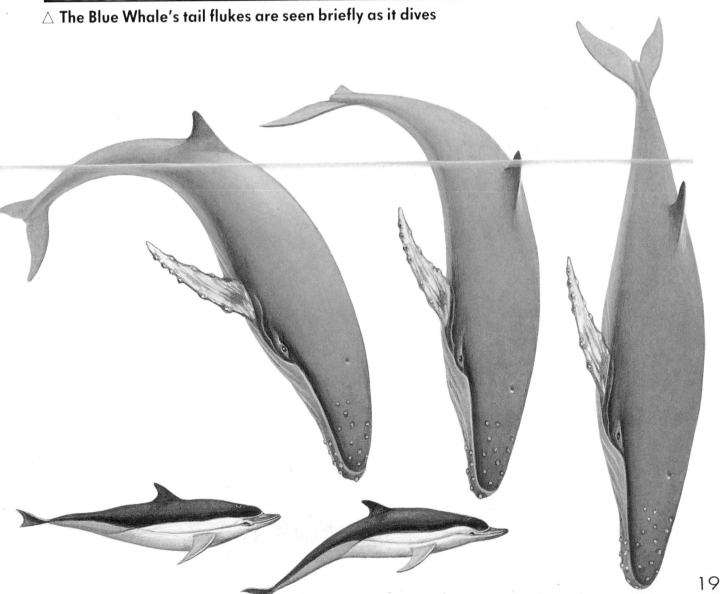

19

Baleen whales

There are two distinct groups of whales, the baleen and the toothed whales. There are ten species of baleen whales. Instead of teeth they have a series of horny plates with fringed edges hanging from the roof of the mouth. These whalebone plates are called the baleen and are used as a sieve for feeding.

Baleen whales feed on animal plankton—krill and tiny creatures that float in the water. Where these swarm, the whale opens its mouth, takes in sea water, then pushes it out through the fringes. The food items are kept back by the fringes and then swallowed. The Blue Whale, the biggest animal that has ever lived, grows to 165 tons on this diet.

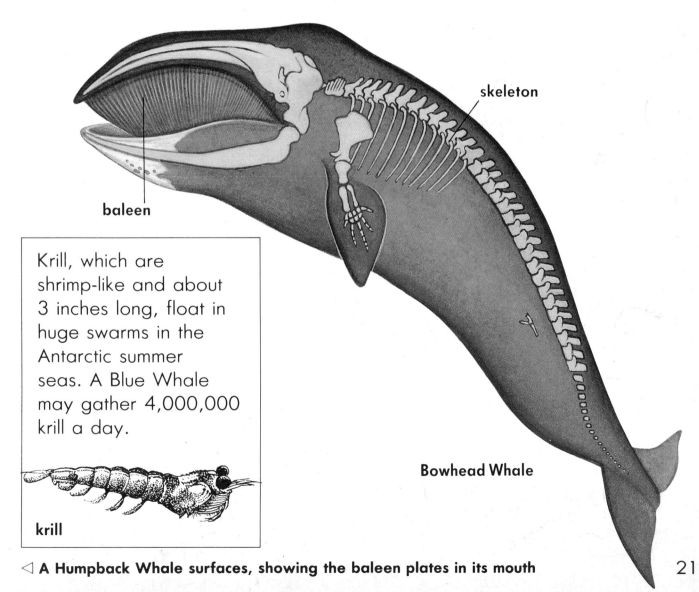

skeleton

baleen

Krill, which are shrimp-like and about 3 inches long, float in huge swarms in the Antarctic summer seas. A Blue Whale may gather 4,000,000 krill a day.

krill

Bowhead Whale

◁ **A Humpback Whale surfaces, showing the baleen plates in its mouth**

Toothed whales

Most of the whales in the world, including all the dolphins, are toothed whales. They have jawbones full of short, cone-shaped teeth, which they use to hold on to slippery prey like fish and squid. The Common Dolphin has more than 200 teeth. The Sperm Whale, and other species that feed on soft-bodied prey like squid, have fewer than 50.

The Killer Whale often eats warm-blooded prey such as penguins, seals and even dolphins. It hunts in packs with the whales working together as a team. Some dolphins, like the Bottlenose Dolphin, also feed as a group. They will round up and capture shoals of fish such as tuna.

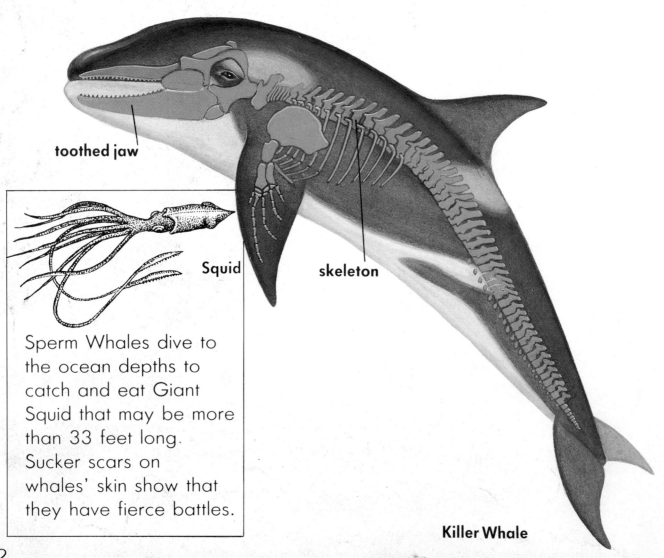

toothed jaw

Squid

skeleton

Sperm Whales dive to the ocean depths to catch and eat Giant Squid that may be more than 33 feet long. Sucker scars on whales' skin show that they have fierce battles.

Killer Whale

22

Dolphins and porpoises

The smaller toothed whales include the unicorn-like Narwhal, the White Beluga, the dolphins and the porpoises. Porpoises have a rounded head, without the beak-like jaw which dolphins have. They grow to only about 5 feet in length. They have a small top fin or none at all.

Dolphins can grow to about 13 feet long and they have a well-developed top fin. The Bottlenose Dolphin and the Common Dolphin are found almost worldwide, except for polar waters. River dolphins live in large tropical rivers like the Amazon and Indus. They are slow swimmers and sometimes use their long "beak" to probe the riverbed for crabs.

Common Dolphin

Common Porpoise

The name porpoise comes from an old Latin word meaning pig-fish. Porpoises feed mainly on fish such as herring. Dolphins eat fish, squid and octopuses. They often live in groups of more than 100 individuals and swim close to land.

The Bottlenose Dolphin prefers to live in groups ▷

Some whales use echolocation to navigate and find prey. They make high-pitched sounds that are directed forward. Echoes bounce back from prey or the sea floor and are picked up by the whale's ears.

sonar

Shortfin Pilot Whale

Senses and sounds

Like us, whales have a pair of eyes and ears, a nose and a tongue. Whales can see quite well in open air and in shallow water. But because they do not have forward-facing eyes, they cannot judge distances very well. When underwater, a whale keeps its nostril closed and so it cannot smell scents. But its tongue can taste chemicals in the water.

Whales do not have large ear openings. But they have excellent hearing and can detect sound waves travelling through the water. Whales make sounds that other whales can hear and respond to. Toothed whales navigate using echolocation, which is similar to the sonar used by ships to navigate.

Beluga Whales ("sea-canaries") have loud and varied voices ▷

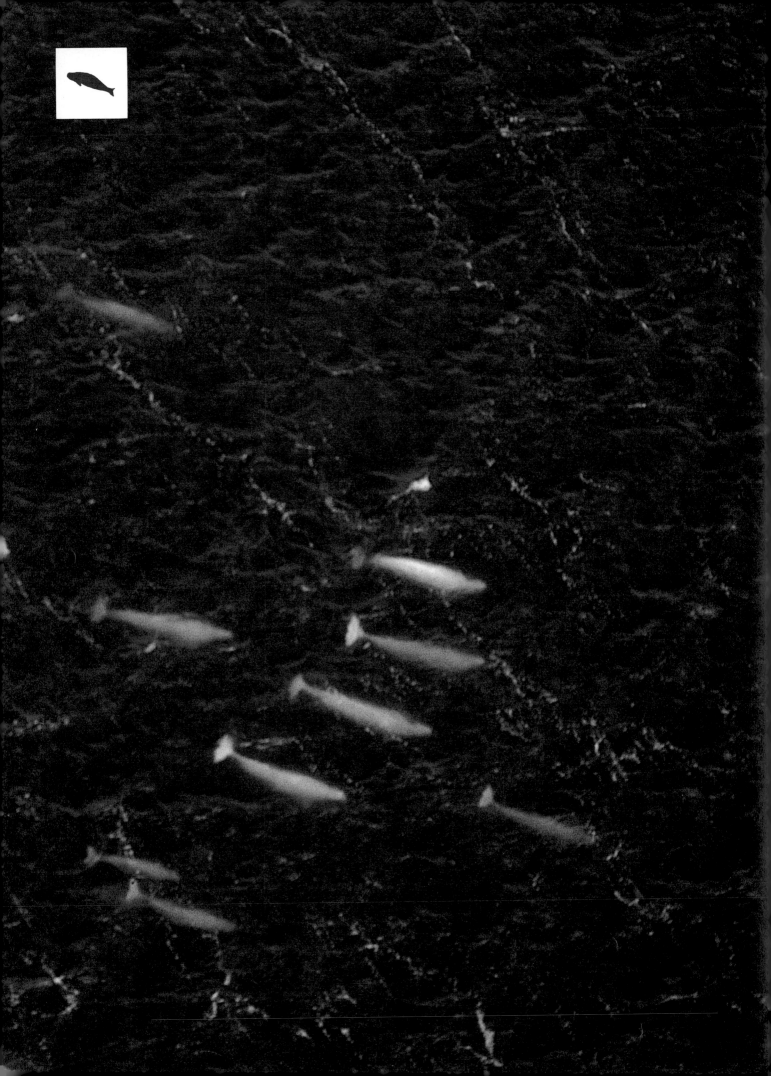

Migration

Throughout the year most toothed whales are constantly on the move, following the shoals of fish they feed on. This may take them on endless circuits round the oceans. By contrast, baleen whales make annual to-and-fro journeys between summer feeding and winter breeding areas.

The plankton on which baleen whales feed is most plentiful in Arctic and Antarctic waters during the summer. The Gray Whale migrates 12,000 miles from far north to breeding grounds off California. Among Blue Whales, there are Northern and Southern Hemisphere populations. Their breeding grounds lie generally on either side of the equator. The populations do not mix.

Migration route of the Gray Whale

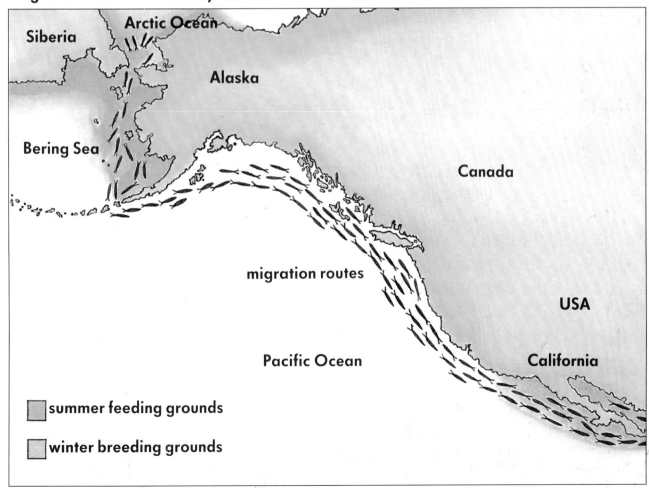

Siberia · Arctic Ocean · Alaska · Bering Sea · Canada · migration routes · Pacific Ocean · USA · California

☐ summer feeding grounds

☐ winter breeding grounds

◁ **Beluga Whales gather in huge herds as they move south in autumn**

A newborn dolphin has no air in its lungs and it tends to sink. Its mother, or her friends, nudge the baby to the surface, where the air stimulates it to open its blowhole and take its first breath. After this it needs no more assistance to breathe or to feed.

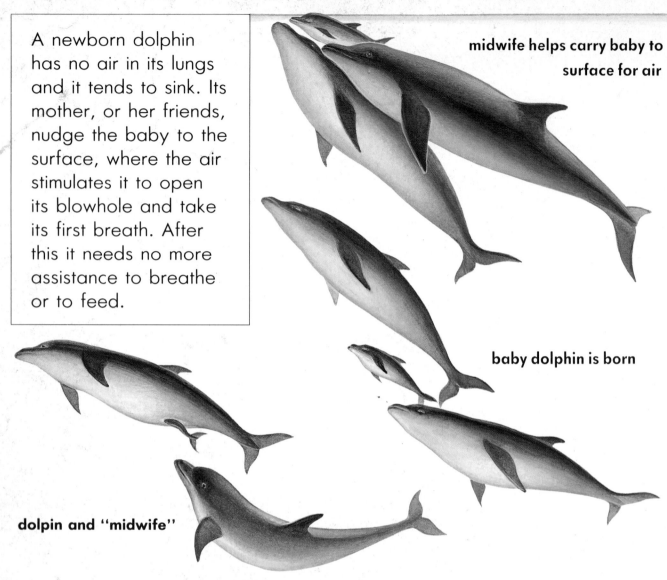

midwife helps carry baby to surface for air

baby dolphin is born

dolpin and "midwife"

Breeding

Before mating, male toothed whales like the Sperm Whale often fight over females, butting and biting each other for the right to mate. Males of all species usually court the females. They chase them through the water, perform displays of splashing and diving, then swim alongside and stroke and caress them with their head. Even large species like the Humpback Whale have energetic courtship displays, ending with the pair rising out of the water to mate face to face.

In baleen whales, courtship and mating take place in warm tropical waters, and the young are born there the following year. In most whales pregnancy lasts for about a year.

A male Gray Whale courts a female underwater ▷

Giant babies

Whales have the biggest babies in the world—a Blue Whale calf may be 25 feet long and weigh 15,400 pounds. They are also some of the fastest-growing young, doubling their weight in the first week. The calves take their first feed a few minutes after birth. When the mother suckles the calf, she pumps milk that is very thick and rich in fat into its mouth.

In big baleen whales like the Humpback, Blue and Gray, the mothers produce milk for about six months. By this time the whales have returned to the summer polar feeding grounds where the young can easily find plankton food. The mother can then replace the blubber that she converted to milk.

◁ **A baby Humpback Whale and its mother**

The Blue Whale may weigh as much as 7.7 tons at birth. It grows rapidly at first. Growth slows as it reaches maturity.

1 day (25 feet)

7 months (53 feet)

5 years old (76 feet)

25 years old (86 feet)

By swimming close to its mother a baby whale gets an easier ride ▷

Intelligence

Dolphins appear to be highly intelligent. They have a language of whistles, chirps, clicks and moans that allows them to communicate with one another over great distances. In captivity they learn tricks and are able to copy many sounds and actions made by people. Some scientists believe that they are more intelligent than dogs, but less so than apes.

Some of a whale's intelligent behavior may just be the result of natural playfulness and friendliness rather than true intelligence. Female whales, for example, automatically help one another to bring up their calves. Dolphins automatically help injured colleagues to the surface to breathe.

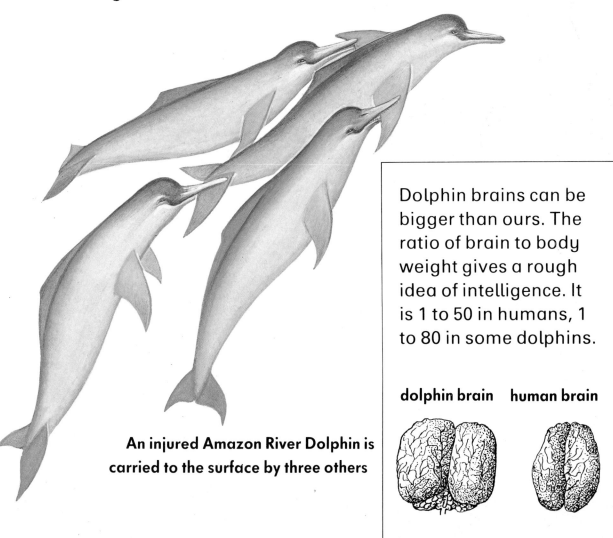

An injured Amazon River Dolphin is carried to the surface by three others

Dolphin brains can be bigger than ours. The ratio of brain to body weight gives a rough idea of intelligence. It is 1 to 50 in humans, 1 to 80 in some dolphins.

dolphin brain   **human brain**

◁ **Dolphins can communicate by sounds**

Survival file

For hundreds of years whales have been hunted and killed. Their flesh is still eaten by many people around the world and is also used to make pet foods. Blubber is the source of whale oil that can be used as a fuel. Smokeless candles, lamps and a lubricant oil for machines can also be made from whale products. The whaling industry has been a ruthless destroyer of wildlife. The numbers of many species have dropped dramatically as animals have been killed faster than they can breed. Today whaling is being halted to let populations grow again.

Whales and dolphins are being studied by scientists

The Right Whales were the first to become rare as they were the "right" (easiest) whales to hunt. Being slow swimmers, they were easily caught by the first sail-powered whaling ships. With the development of engine-powered whaling ships and explosive harpoons, all whales became easy targets for the hunters. Then it was the Sperm Whale and the big baleen whales that suffered. In 1931 thirty thousand Blue Whales were killed in the Antarctic. Never again have so many been seen. There are probably little more than ten thousand left in the whole world.

The explosive harpoon made it easier to catch and kill big whales

Dolphins are also hunted for meat in some parts of Southeast Asia and South America. Many others die trapped in fishing nets.

Conservation measures and falling profits have brought whaling to a standstill in certain countries. But whaling still continues in other parts of the world. For many species numbers have fallen so low that their recovery is now in doubt. Often little is known about how they live. It is only in the last thirty years that dolphins and small whales have been studied in captivity.

Killer Whales in a marine park

Identification chart

This chart shows about one-fifth of the world's different species of whales and dolphins and indicates where they live. They are drawn to scale. Each section of the grid represents 6.6 feet. The Bottlenose Dolphin is the most frequently seen in zoos.

○ North Atlantic
● South Atlantic
● North Pacific
● South Pacific
● Indian Ocean
● Rivers

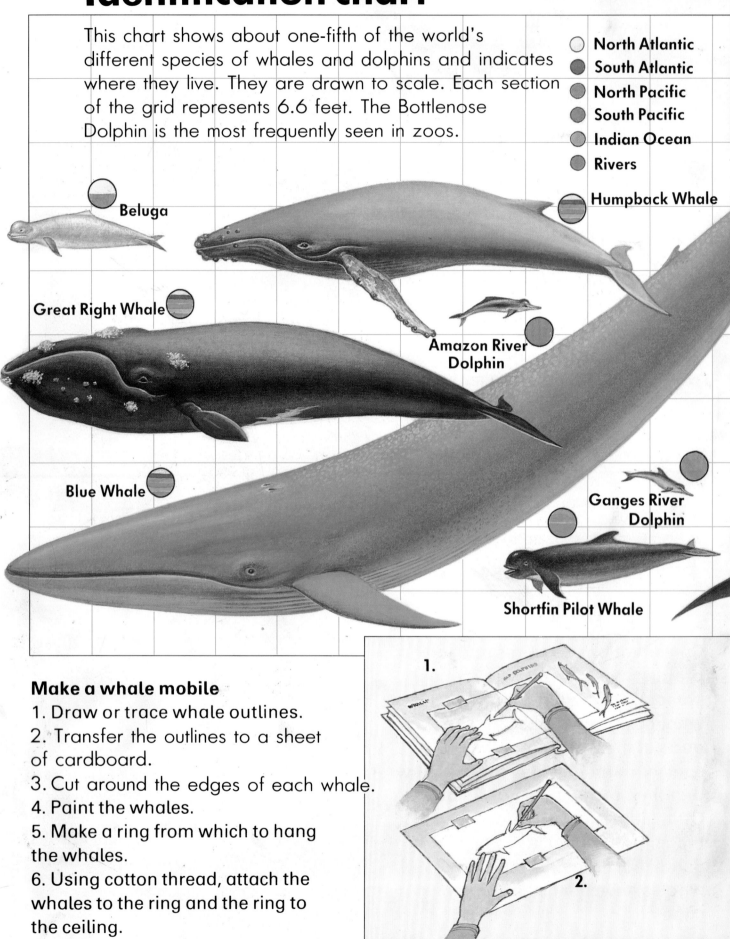

Beluga

Humpback Whale

Great Right Whale

Amazon River Dolphin

Blue Whale

Ganges River Dolphin

Shortfin Pilot Whale

Make a whale mobile
1. Draw or trace whale outlines.
2. Transfer the outlines to a sheet of cardboard.
3. Cut around the edges of each whale.
4. Paint the whales.
5. Make a ring from which to hang the whales.
6. Using cotton thread, attach the whales to the ring and the ring to the ceiling.

1.

2.

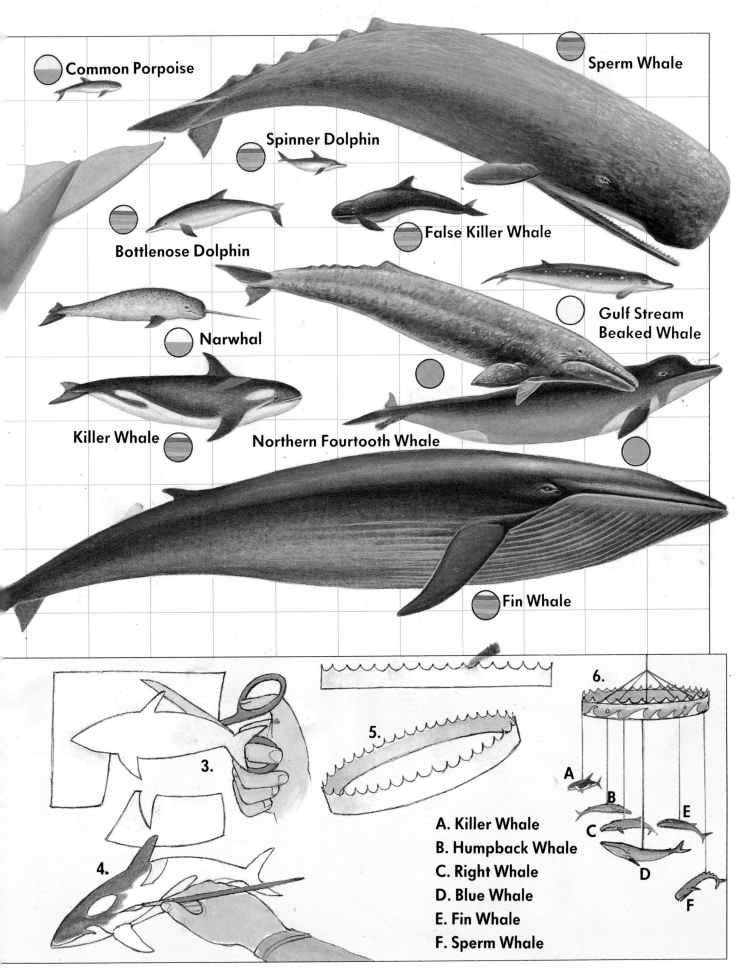

Common Porpoise

Sperm Whale

Spinner Dolphin

Bottlenose Dolphin

False Killer Whale

Gulf Stream
Beaked Whale

Narwhal

Killer Whale

Northern Fourtooth Whale

Fin Whale

3.

4.

5.

6.

A. Killer Whale
B. Humpback Whale
C. Right Whale
D. Blue Whale
E. Fin Whale
F. Sperm Whale

A
B
C
D
E
F

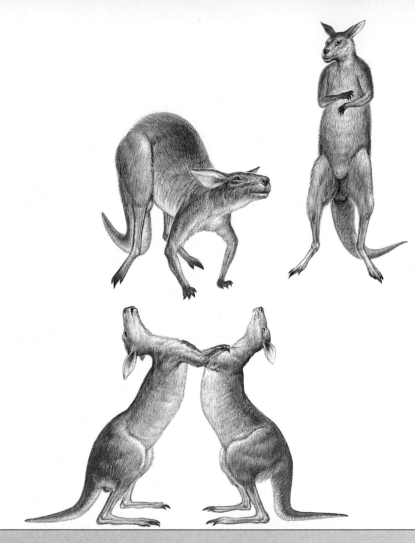

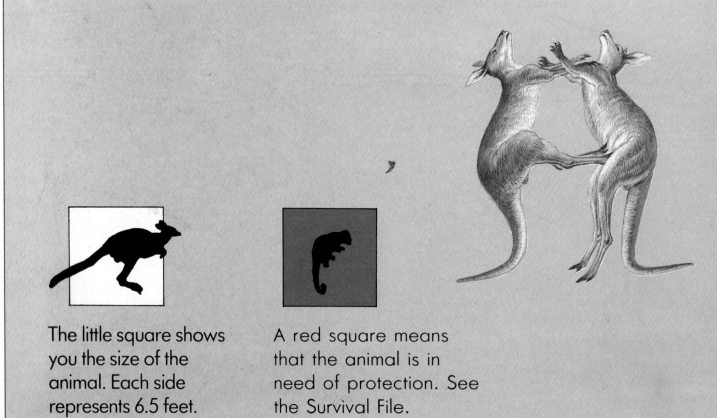

The little square shows you the size of the animal. Each side represents 6.5 feet.

A red square means that the animal is in need of protection. See the Survival File.

The picture opposite shows a possum sitting on a tree trunk

Chapter 2
KANGAROOS
AND OTHER
MARSUPIALS

Lionel Bender

Facts to Know

Kangaroos are mammals, as we are. But unlike us, the newborn look nothing like their parents. After they are born they grow in a pouch outside their mother's belly. Pouched mammals are known as marsupials.

The kangaroo family includes three species of true kangaroo and 47 similar, smaller species known as wallabies. All members of the kangaroo family live in Australia and the islands nearby. They feed on grass and other plants, and inhabit grasslands and forests. In the same part of the world there are about 120 other species of marsupials. These include the Koala, wombats and the possums. There are also pouched mammals living in America. They are called opossums. There are about 80 species of opossum.

◁ **The Red Kangaroo is the largest marsupial**

Pouched animals

The largest pouched mammal, the Red Kangaroo, grows to $6\frac{1}{2}$ feet long and 200 pounds in weight. But at birth, it is only $\frac{3}{4}$ inch long and weighs about $\frac{1}{30}$ ounce. The baby is born after developing inside its mother's womb for only five weeks. It spends the next six months inside her pouch feeding on milk.

The babies of most mammals grow and develop inside their mother's body until they are fully formed. They get all their food from a special structure inside the womb called a placenta. But female marsupials do not have placentas. Their babies must come out of the womb when very small and suckle milk constantly until they can look after themselves.

Pouched mammals have lifestyles like those of placental mammals. Kangaroos, for example, feed and behave like the antelope of Africa. There are pouched mammals that look exactly like placental mammals, such as wolves, cats and house mice.

marsupial mouse

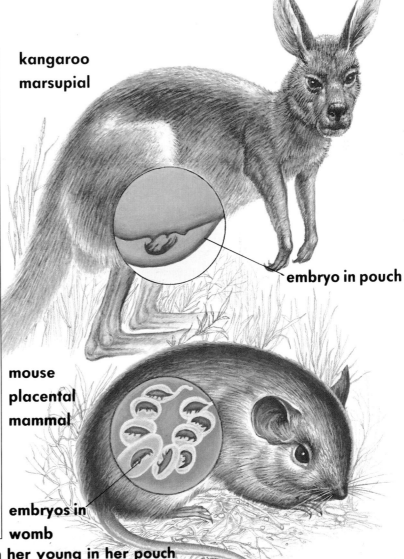

kangaroo marsupial

embryo in pouch

mouse placental mammal

embryos in womb

◁ **A mother Gray Kangaroo with her young in her pouch**

45

Hopping along

Kangaroos and most wallabies are built for hopping on two legs and not for walking or running. They stand upright, using their long tails as a third foot and their long, powerful hind legs as springboards. The scientific name for kangaroos is *Macropus*, meaning great foot – they have extremely long feet. When hopping, they use their tails for balance and as rudders to help them turn in the air.

Kangaroos graze rather like sheep, moving about slowly in search of grass to eat and water to drink. They move a yard at a time from place to place. But when they are frightened or being chased, they can make great leaps and travel fast and far.

Wallaby skeleton

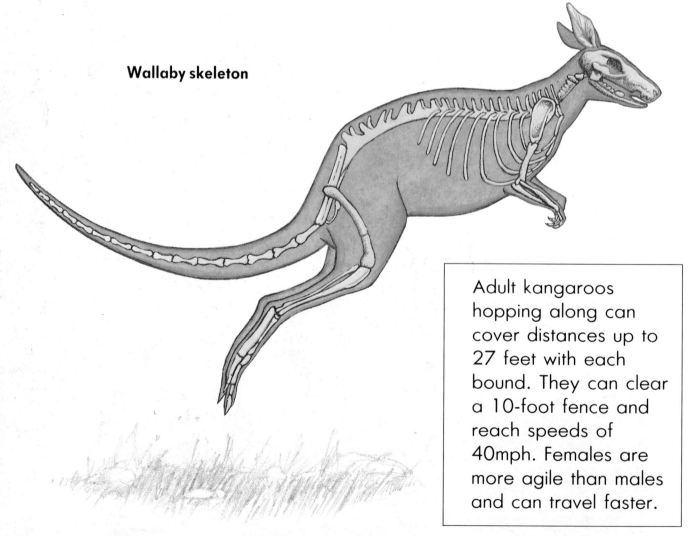

Adult kangaroos hopping along can cover distances up to 27 feet with each bound. They can clear a 10-foot fence and reach speeds of 40mph. Females are more agile than males and can travel faster.

A wallaby hops along ▷

Glider

Climbers, gliders and burrowers

Tree kangaroos and the Koala live in forests. They are built for climbing, not hopping. Their front and back pairs of legs are almost the same length. With their back legs, these marsupials can cling to and push themselves up tree trunks. They move among the trees, grasping the branches with their strong hands.

Gliders are pouched mammals that live in woodlands and forests. They have flaps of furred skin stretched between their front and back legs. With the flaps outstretched, the animals can glide 330 feet between treetops. But gliders do not land gently. They bump into trees at quite high speeds. They use their long claws to fasten onto the trees.

Marsupial Mole

◁ **A Koala climbing in a eucalyptus tree**

Other marsupials are burrowers. The marsupial mole burrows underground to feed on insect larvae. It has stubby limbs and claws for scraping and pushing away soil.

Plant-eaters

The Koala, which grows to 24 inches tall and
22 pounds in weight, is a very fussy eater. It will only eat
the leaves of eucalyptus trees. It feeds from dusk
onwards, and in a single night it eats up to 2 pounds of
leaves. It sometimes stores food in its cheek pouches
and dozes off to sleep during a meal.

Wombats have gnawing teeth like a squirrel's. They
live in burrows by day and come out at night to feed
on grasses, bark and fungi. Some possums and
gliders make notches in the bark of trees with their
teeth and lick up the sweet, sugary gum. Others feed
on the pollen and nectar of forest flowers. Marsupials
such as the Spotted Cuscus of New Guinea eat insects,
birds and their eggs, as well as plants.

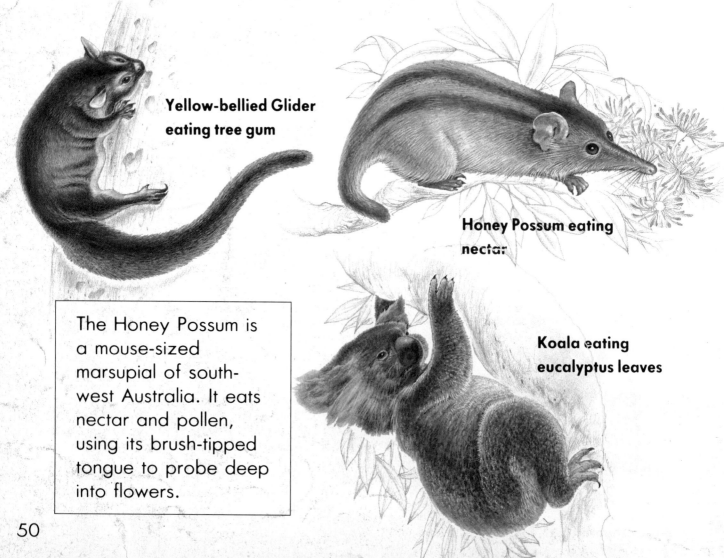

**Yellow-bellied Glider
eating tree gum**

**Honey Possum eating
nectar**

**Koala eating
eucalyptus leaves**

The Honey Possum is
a mouse-sized
marsupial of south-
west Australia. It eats
nectar and pollen,
using its brush-tipped
tongue to probe deep
into flowers.

Meat-eaters

Many different types of pouched mammals feed on the flesh of other animals. They include the 80 species of American opossums, the bandicoots and Numbat of Australia, and the Tasmanian Devil.

Marsupial carnivores are often called cats. This is because, like true cats, they are hunters and have pointed canine teeth and sharp claws. But the Pilbara Ningaui is a marsupial that is mouse-like in both size and looks, and it feeds on insects. The Spotted-tailed Quoll looks like a weasel, and it feeds on small wallabies. The Tasmanian Devil, which grows to 35 inches from head to tail, often hunts lambs and chickens, but prefers to scavenge on dead animals.

The Pilbara Ningaui eats insects

An antechinus eats small lizards

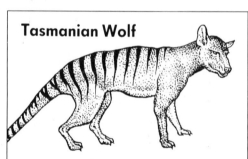

Tasmanian Wolf

The Tasmanian Wolf was a dog-like pouched mammal that was found all over Tasmania about 100 years ago. It has since been hunted to extinction. It was about 24 inches high and about 32 inches long.

Wombats live in underground homes 20 inches wide and 100 feet long. They feed at night. In winter the Common Wombat, which lives in heaths and on hills, comes out during the day to warm up in the sun.

Wombat burrowing

Daily life

Most marsupials feed at night and rest during the day. The Koala, for example, spends the daytime sleeping, wedged between branches of a eucalyptus tree. At sunset, it climbs to the treetop to feed. Cuscuses, possums and opossums move through forests at night, travelling between feeding and resting sites.

In hot weather, kangaroos feed at dawn and again late at night. They spend the daytime sleeping and sheltering from the sun under trees. In cooler weather, they feed during the day and sleep at night. The Colocolo, a small South American marsupial, lives in cool, damp forests. In winter it hibernates in nests in hollow trees or under tree roots.

A possum feeding in a tree at night ▷

Social life

Kangaroos live in groups called mobs. A mob usually consists of an adult male and two or three females and their young. The young are known as joeys. A baby joey will stay with its mother until it is about 20 months old. Then, every week or two, it may move from one mob to another. When food is easy to find, mobs collect together in groups of 50 or more.

The Koala and most other marsupials live alone. They only seek the company of others at mating time. A male Koala may attract two or three females and mate with each of them. A mother Koala looks after her young until it is about a year old. She carries the youngster on her back as she moves through the trees.

A mob of Red Kangaroos feeding

A young kangaroo looks and listens for its mother ▷

Enemies and defense

Kangaroos have several deadly enemies. The fiercest is the Dingo, the native Australian dog. Only a fully grown kangaroo can match the Dingo's fighting skills. When cornered, a kangaroo will kick with its hind legs and use its claws to rip at its enemy's flesh. Joey kangaroos are often preyed on by eagles and foxes. The Koala is also killed by Dingos and by large lizards.

Many of the small marsupials, such as bandicoots, can scurry away quickly when danger threatens. Most of them go unnoticed, however, because their fur is colored to blend in with their background. Opossums act dead, or "play possum," when in danger. As most hunting animals prefer to kill their victims, they leave the opossums alone.

Dingos are the size of a collie. They are placental mammals. They hunt alone, in pairs, or in small packs. They prey on all kinds of marsupial. They creep up on their victims and then pounce. They live in the forests and open grasslands of central Australia.

The Dingo

Eastern Barred Bandicoot

◁ **A kangaroo escapes from a pack of dingos**

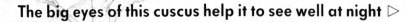

At mating time, a male Koala attracts females and warns off other males with growling calls that sound like a chain saw. A female Koala that is not ready to mate uses a wailing distress call to discourage males.

A male and female Sugar Glider rub each other with their body scents so that they will be able to recognize one another

Senses and scents

A marsupial's most important senses are hearing and smell. Kangaroos have long ear flaps, which they can turn backwards and forwards to hear sounds from all directions. Antechinuses and other meat-eaters that hunt at night use hearing to locate and home in on their prey. Most tree-dwellers use sounds to keep in touch with one another at a distance.

Possums and gliders live in a world of smells and body scents. They mark their areas with their urine and dung, and rub one another with scents from their skin glands. Brushtail possums and cuscuses rely more on vision than hearing for their survival in the forests. They have large, forward-facing eyes that help them judge distances accurately.

Courtship and breeding

Female kangaroos are ready to mate and have babies when they are about 18 months old. Male kangaroos are about 3½ years old before they can mate. Generally, kangaroos mate in summer so that the joeys are ready to leave the pouch the following spring.

Male kangaroos often fight with one another for the right to mate with a female. The winner then courts the female by nuzzling her and wooing her with clucking noises. The pair then mate. The female produces just one baby at a time. As soon as the baby is born, it makes its way to its mother's pouch and searches for one of her four teats to get milk. The mother is then ready to mate again.

Female Virginia Opossums produce up to 50 young at a time. But most of these die as they never find their way to one of their mother's 13 tiny teats.

Reproduction of the Red Kangaroo

The baby suckles in the pouch. The mother mates again two days after the first birth.

The first joey suckles less as it grows.

A mother Koala and her infant rest in a tree during the day

A second baby is born after the first joey has left the pouch (seven months after it was born).

The first joey now eats plant food, but still suckles. The second joey suckles constantly.

Growing up

A newborn kangaroo has no ears, no eyes and no fur. It looks more like a baby mouse than a kangaroo. Using the claws on its tiny front limbs, it climbs into its mother's pouch. This 6-inch journey takes about three minutes. Here it gets food, warmth and protection. When it is about five months old, the joey pokes its head out of the pouch for the first time. Over the next few months, it leaves the pouch for longer periods each day. It starts to hop, to feed on grass and to clean itself. But whenever it is frightened, it pops back into its mother's pouch.

Joeys are very playful. They wrestle and box with one another. This is good practice for defending themselves against dingos and foxes. It is also practice for male kangaroos, which fight to win females when they are adult. Kangaroos live for up to 18 years in the wild and 28 years in captivity.

A newborn kangaroo must find its way to one of it's mother's teats and quickly start to take milk, otherwise it dies. It gets no help from its mother. As it suckles, the teat swells and fills its mouth. This means the mother cannot dislodge her young when she moves around. The baby grows quickly, but it is a month or more before it starts to look like its parents.

Young Red Kangaroos fighting

The two opponents approach one another, stalking about and scratching as if preparing for battle.

Opossum babies on their mother's back

They lock their forearms together and wrestle.

Then they try and push each other to the ground.

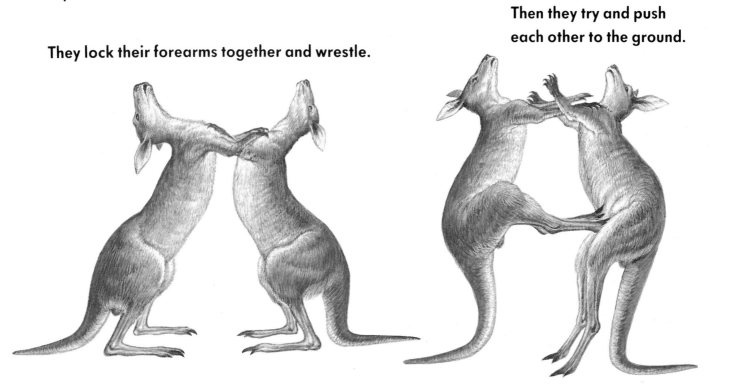

Survival file

In Australia, marsupials have suffered greatly since the arrival of European people in the 1770s. Before then the native Aborigines hunted most species of marsupial for meat, but they never killed large numbers of the animals. The Europeans brought with them sheep, cattle, rabbits, foxes, cats and dogs, and they cleared forests to graze their animals. The kangaroos ate much of the grass that the farmers needed for their sheep and cattle, so they were regarded as pests and shot in the thousands.

An abandoned joey is rescued after its mother has been killed

Until the 1930s, the Koala and other marsupials were shot for sport. Others were killed for their fur. As forests were cut down, the homes of tree-living species such as the cuscuses and brushtail possums were destroyed. All marsupials became easy prey to foxes, or to cats and dogs that became wild.

In South America, the greatest threat to the opossums was, and still is, the destruction of their forest homes. In North America, however, opossums are not endangered, despite being hunted for food and their fur. Many live on farms and in towns. The Virginia Opossum can now be found as far north as Canada.

Koalas are removed from the wild to protected areas

Kangaroos are sometimes killed to keep their numbers down

Hunting of marsupials is largely forbidden today in Australia. The Koala live mainly in special reserves, and there are protected areas of temperate and tropical forests where most species are able to live freely. The large Red, Gray and Hill Kangaroos, however, sometimes roam *too* freely over the open grasslands. Occasionally they have to be shot or poisoned in large numbers to keep their populations at reasonable levels.

Identification chart

This chart shows you a wide variety of pouched mammals, most of which can be seen in zoos. They range in size from the Red Kangaroo to the Woolly Opossum and the Sugar Glider. Notice how only the kangaroos and wallabies are built for hopping along. Each square represents 12 inches.

◯ **Australian species**

◯ **American species**

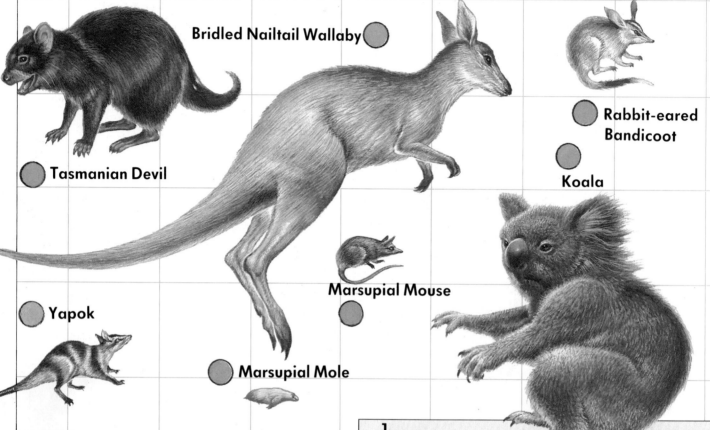

Bridled Nailtail Wallaby

Tasmanian Devil

Rabbit-eared Bandicoot

Koala

Yapok

Marsupial Mouse

Marsupial Mole

Make the Marsupial Game

1. Draw and color board as shown. Number squares 1 to 100.
2. Make counters using cardboard.
3. Write out question cards using the table provided. Add more of your own animals to the list.
4. To play, take turns to throw the dice and move forwards, starting from 1. Each time you land on a colored square, take a question card. If you get the correct answer, move on 4 squares. If you get it wrong, go back 4.

1.

91	92	93	94	95		97	98	99	100
90	89	88	87	86	85	84	83	82	81
71	72	73	74	75	76	77	78	79	80
70	69	68	67	66	65	64	63	62	61
51	52	53	54	55	56	57	58	59	60
50	49	48	47	46	45	44	43	42	41
31	32	33	34	35	36	37	38	39	40
30	29	28	27	26	25	24	23	22	21
11	12	13	14	15	16	7	18	19	20
10	9	8	7	6	5	4	3	2	1

Sugar Glider

Spotted Cuscus

Red Kangaroo

Brush-tailed Possum

Woolly Opossum

Common Wombat

Bennett's Tree Kangaroo

2. counters

Animal	Is it a marsupial?	Animal	Is it a marsupial?
Red Kangaroo	Yes	Rock Wallaby	Yes
Cuscus	Yes	Striped Possum	Yes
Wallaby	Yes	Tiger Cat	Yes
Capybara	No	Impala	No
Bandicoot	Yes	Mongoose	No
Golden Jackal	No	Cicada	No
Maned Wolf	No	Platypus	No
Long-eared Bat	No	Flying Fox	No
Kangaroo Rat	No	Tiger	No
Mole	No	Potto	No
Tasmanian Wolf	Yes	Flying Phalanger	Yes
Virginia Opossum	Yes		
Tasmanian Devil	Yes		
Koala	Yes		
Quoll	Yes		
Sugar Glider	Yes		
Dingo	No		
Yapok	Yes		
Leadbeater's Opossum	Yes		
Wombat	Yes		
Numbat	Yes		
Star-nosed Mole	No		
Dunnart	Yes		
Tree Kangaroo	Yes		
Dasyure Cat	Yes		
Jerboa	No		
Common Marmot	No		

3.

NUMBAT

YES

The little square shows you how big the animal is compared to a person. Each side represents 9 feet.

A red square means that it is endangered in all or part of its range. See the Survival File.

The picture opposite shows an Arctic Fox pup in its winter coat

Chapter 3
POLAR ANIMALS
Lionel Bender

Facts to Know

The areas around the North and South Poles are covered in ice, snow and cold water. The climate there is bleak and hostile. Even in summer the temperature only rises to about 46°F above zero, and in winter it can fall to 94°F below. Yet many animals live in these regions. Most species have a thick coat or a layer of fat to protect them from the cold. Some animals spend the coldest months asleep in dens beneath the snow. Others are just summer visitors.

All polar animals depend on the plants that grow in the seas or on the land during the summer. Some, such as seals, feed in the water but still rest and breed on the shore. Here many of them are killed and eaten by land animals like Polar Bears and Arctic Foxes.

◁ **The Musk-ox has a coat of dense soft wool and thick hair**

North and south

The two polar regions are at opposite ends of the Earth. The northern region is known as the Arctic, and the southern region, the Antarctic. The Arctic is an area of frozen ocean surrounded by large masses of land. Animals such as the Caribou, Musk-ox and Arctic Hare live there. They all feed on land plants, and are a source of food for meat-eaters like the Polar Bear and the Wolf. The Beluga, Narwhal, Walrus and several species of seal live in the cold Arctic seas.

The Antarctic is a mass of land permanently buried beneath a great sheet of ice. In this polar region the biggest land animals are insects! But the world's largest animal, the Blue Whale, lives in the icy waters. Huge populations of penguins, sea lions and fur seals also feed along the edge of the ice sheet.

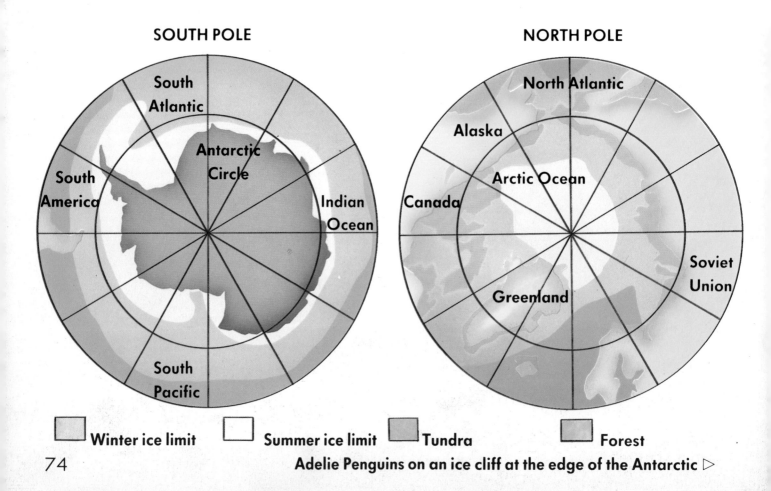

SOUTH POLE

South Atlantic

Antarctic Circle

South America

Indian Ocean

South Pacific

NORTH POLE

North Atlantic

Alaska

Arctic Ocean

Canada

Soviet Union

Greenland

☐ Winter ice limit   ☐ Summer ice limit   ☐ Tundra   ☐ Forest

Adelie Penguins on an ice cliff at the edge of the Antarctic ▷

Polar Bears

The Polar Bear is the largest and strongest hunter in the Arctic. A fully grown male may measure 9 feet in length and weigh 1,000 pounds. The bear's favorite food is seals, which it stuns with a blow from one of its huge front paws and then tears apart with its teeth and claws. But Polar Bears also eat fish, birds and their eggs, and scraps of food thrown away by people.

In October, as winter approaches, a pregnant female Polar Bear carves out a den deep in the snow. She spends the cold months here, giving birth to her cubs in December. The newborn cubs feed on mother's milk until they are six months old. All the bears leave the den in March or April. Soon after, the young start to eat meat.

Polar Bears are good swimmers. When they go into icy cold waters, their thick, oily fur and a layer of fat beneath the skin keep them warm. They paddle with their front legs and use their hind legs as a rudder to steer. Polar Bears can swim steadily for many hours to get from one ice floe to another.

Polar Bear swimming

Cross-section of a Polar Bear den

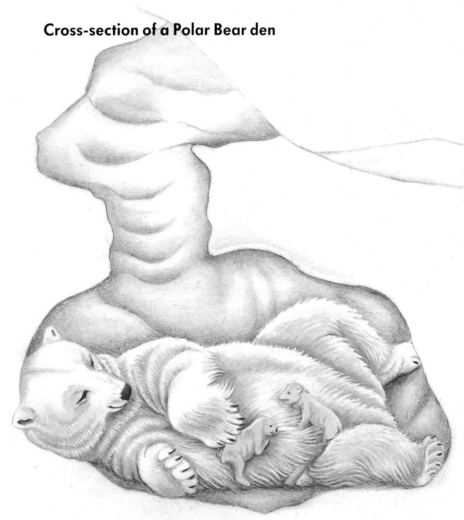

◁ **A Polar Bear mother and her two cubs venture across the ice**

Predators and prey

Some Arctic meat-eaters such as the Wolf and Lynx are predators – they hunt and kill other animals. The animals they hunt, called their prey, range from Reindeer and Musk-ox to Arctic Hare and Lemmings. Other meat-eaters like the Wolverine (also called the Glutton) are scavengers. They steal the kills of predators and feed on any dead animals they find.

Birds of prey such as the Golden Eagle and the Snowy Owl hunt from the air. They feed on small mammals and birds that live and breed in the far north. The birds fly low over the ground in search of food, swooping down to catch and kill animals with their talons. They rip their prey apart with their hooked beaks.

Musk-oxen grouped together to protect themselves from a pack of wolves

Musk-oxen are easy prey for hunters as they do not run away when attacked. Instead, the adults form a protective circle, keeping their young in the middle and facing outwards.

A Wolverine defends its food and territory aggressively

A Golden Eagle stands guard over a dead deer

Male Walruses fighting

Life on the ice

Walruses live on ice floes, sometimes far out to sea. They spend a lot of time in the water, plowing the seabed with their long upper teeth, or tusks, for clams. They eat the flesh of these animals after sucking it from the shells with their thick, muscular lips. When they are not feeding, Walruses rest or sleep on ice floes or beaches. To haul themselves out of the water, they dig their tusks into the ice and "walk on their teeth" until safely ashore. Walruses also use their tusks as weapons against predators such as Killer Whales, or to keep open a breathing hole in the ice.

Like all penguins, the Adelie Penguin is a flightless bird that lives in the Antarctic. It uses its wings as paddles and to help it leap up onto ice floes. Adelie Penguins feed on tiny animals called krill.

Walruses "walking on their teeth"

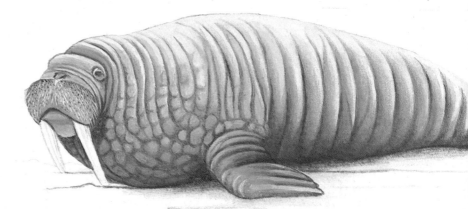

◁ **Gentoo Penguins wandering in the Antarctic snowscape**

Under the snow and ice

Baby Ringed Seals are born in April in snow caves hollowed out by their mothers. The snow keeps the young seals safe from predators such as Arctic Foxes and Polar Bears. It also keeps the seals warm until they have developed a thick insulating layer of fat, or blubber. At first their coat is white. But by the time they are one month old it has taken on a grey, blotchy look. The rings on the coat that gave the seals their name become more distinct as they get older.

Ringed Seals are found throughout the Arctic. They feed on fish and shelled animals like shrimp and crabs. Like all seals, they have to come to the surface of the water to breathe. When the seas freeze over, they scratch and butt at the ice to make air holes.

The Narwhal lives among drifting ice floes in the Arctic Ocean. Males develop a slender tusk up to 10 feet long.

Ringed Seal with young in hollow in snow. The animals breathe through an air hole.

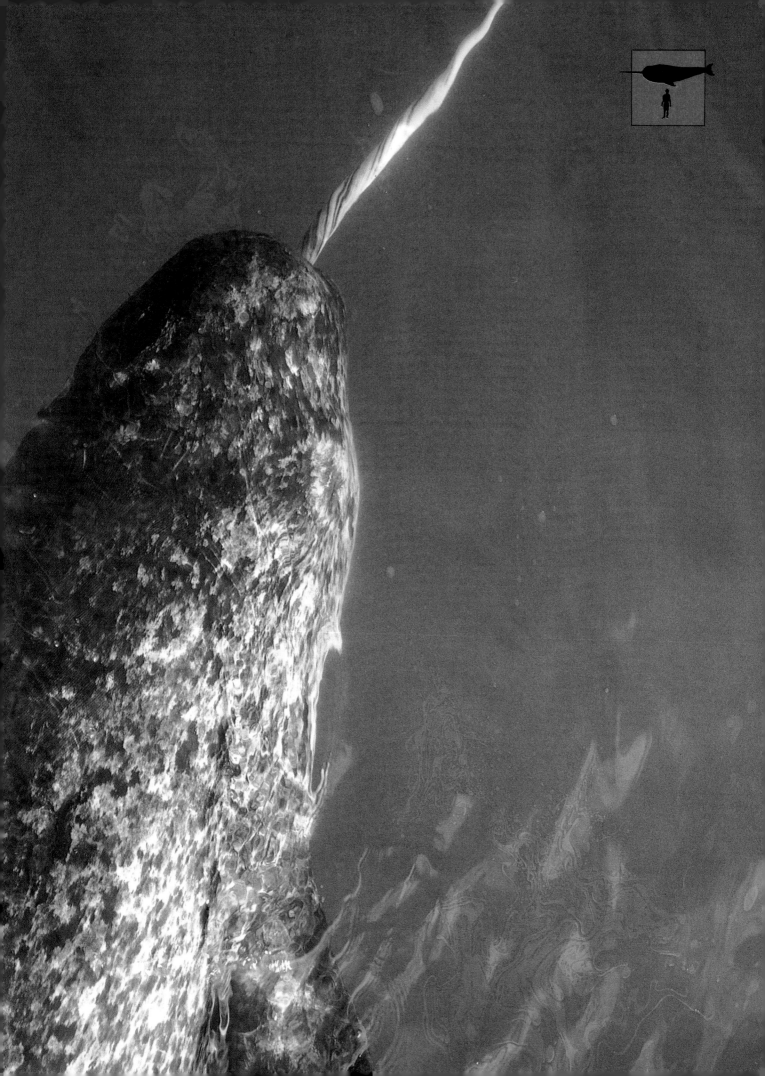

Wilson's Petrel feeding on plankton

King Eider Duck

Food from the water

In the summer, the Arctic and Antarctic seas teem with life. Tiny plants, the phytoplankton, drift in the water. These plants are the main food for animals such as krill, which look like tiny shrimp. Krill are eaten in huge quantities by whales, seals, fish and seabirds.

The treeless Arctic landscape, called the tundra, is also home to many animals. The tundra contains thousands of lakes, marshes, mud flats and estuaries. In the spring, these watery areas are filled with weeds, algae, insect larvae and fish. This aquatic life is a source of food for birds like ducks, geese, swans and divers. Most of these birds breed and nest on the tundra.

The Humpback Whale filters small animals such as krill from the Arctic waters. It does this with the sieve-like plates, called baleen plates, that hang down on either side of its mouth. For this reason it is known as a baleen whale.

Loon diving for fish

◁ **A Humpback Whale "breaching," leaping out of the water**

At the water's edge

For Southern Elephant seals, September and October are the busiest months of the year. This is the start of the Antarctic spring, when the seals come ashore to breed. The males land first and battle with one another for areas of the beach. The females follow a few weeks later. They gather in groups around the winning males. Pups from the last year's mating are soon born and their mothers mate again a week or so later.

In the spring, water birds nest and breed in the millions along the edges of Arctic lakes. Bewick's Swans build a mound of water plants up to 10 feet across. Canada Geese lay their eggs in hollows lined with leaves, grass and down that they pluck from their own breasts.

A nesting Bewick's Swan with its young, or "cygnet"

Young male Elephant Seals in a playful contest ▷

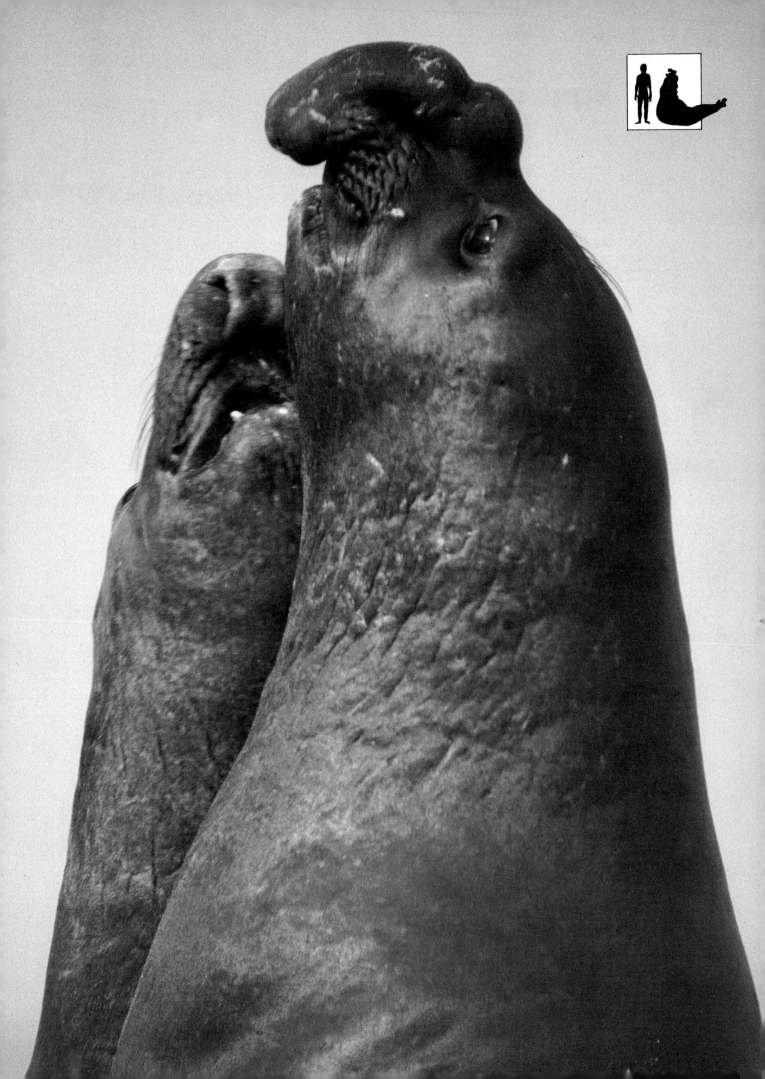

Eggs and young

Female Emperor Penguins lay a single egg, which they carry on their feet. They cover the egg with a fold of skin to keep it warm. After a few days, the fathers take over incubating the eggs and the mothers waddle off across the ice to feed in the water. They return eight weeks later, just as hatching starts, with their stomachs full of partly digested fish and squid.

The mother penguins feed the chicks while the hungry males go off to feed themselves. The chicks venture into the water in December, when food is most plentiful in the Antarctic. By the time they are fully grown the Emperor Penguins will stand almost 3 feet tall and weigh 100 pounds.

Emperor Penguin with chick

Arctic Terns nest in the far north. Both parents look after the chicks, which are born fully-feathered and can swim when only a few days old. The main food of Arctic Terns is fish. The birds hover just above the ocean's surface, then dive into the water and grasp their prey in their beaks. Arctic Terns spend one summer in the Arctic and the next in the Antarctic – six months later.

An Arctic Tern looks after its newborn chick ▷

Color changes

The Rock Ptarmigan is a bird that lives in the tundra and mountains of the north. It feeds on Arctic plants and is eaten by foxes and birds of prey. In the summer the bird's plumage is mottled brown, which blends in well with surrounding rocks and lichens. In the autumn, its coloring gradually changes to pure white. This protects the Rock Ptarmigan from predators by making it difficult to see against the snow.

The Arctic Hare and Arctic Fox also change color with the seasons. Both have a grayish-brown summer coat and a white winter coat. But while the hare's winter coloring helps it to escape predators, the fox's allows it to stay concealed while it hunts other animals.

Stoat in summer

The Stoat is an Arctic predator that has two coats – and two names. In the autumn, its red-brown fur changes to white. The animal is then called an Ermine.

Ermine in winter

The Rock Ptarmigan's winter plumage blends in with the snow...

. . . while its summer feathers are the color of the tundra rocks and plants

Migrations

As summer approaches, many birds and mammals travel great distances to the polar regions. They go to feed on the plants that burst into growth as the long warm days begin. In Canada, huge herds of Caribou migrate 600 miles or more to the Arctic tundra. Their young are born in June. In August, as winter draws near, the whole herd starts the journey south to the forests where they will spend the winter.

In the Antarctic, seabirds like albatrosses, gulls and petrels constantly roam the seas. They feed on the fish, krill and squid that live in the huge southern oceans. Wandering Albatrosses may spend several years at sea. The adult birds travel once or twice around the vast ice cap before coming ashore to breed.

Lemmings live in the far north of Canada, Scandinavia and Siberia. In the winter they live in tunnels beneath the snow. They mainly breed in the summer. Every three or four years their populations become too large for the food supply. When this happens, groups of thousands of lemmings migrate together to find new homes and sources of food. Many of them die on the way.

Norwegian Lemmings on the move

Migrating Caribou herds can contain up to 50,000 animals ▷

Insects

Insects thrive during the short polar summers. In the Antarctic they live on the few plants that grow in sunny, sheltered places. Water Beetles and Mosquito larvae live in Arctic pools and lakes. Mosquitoes are a major pest to some mammals. Huge swarms of them follow the Caribou herds, feeding on the animals' blood.

Insects called Springtails have survived in Arctic ice for as long as three years. Other insects contain an antifreeze that prevents the liquids in their bodies from turning to ice in the winter. But most polar insects hibernate, or pass the winter in a resting stage. They become active again as soon as the snows melt.

A female Mosquito on a tundra rock

94

A Small Copper Butterfly sucks nectar from an Arctic flower ▷

Survival file

People have lived in the Arctic region for thousands of years. The best-known are the Eskimos, or Inuit, of North America and Greenland, and the Lapps of northern Scandinavia and the Soviet Union. The Inuit hunt seals and whales to eat, but only kill as many as they need to support themselves. Some Inuit and Indians also still follow the migrating Caribou herds. In the past, they moved with the herds on sledges pulled by Husky Dogs. Today, many Inuit use motorized sledges or snowmobiles. The Lapps look after tame herds of Reindeer, another name for Caribou. They rely on these animals for food (milk, cheese and meat), transport and clothing.

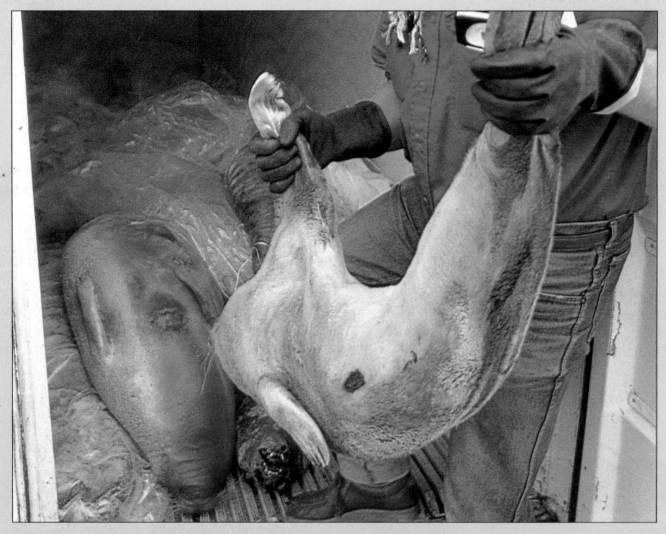

These diseased seals were found washed up on a Danish beach

The Antarctic was not inhabited until the 1800s. At that time explorers, and later whalers and fur trappers, began to arrive. Since then, the wildlife in both polar regions has been seriously threatened by man. Most species of whales have been hunted almost to extinction for their blubber, meat and oils. Seals, Polar Bears, Arctic Foxes and Stoats have all been killed for their fur. Walruses and Narwhals were hunted for their ivory tusks.

A Lapp with his Reindeer herd

Both polar regions have been badly damaged and polluted in the last hundred years. This has happened because of oil and mineral exploration, the construction of roads and airstrips, and the use of vehicles that can travel over snow and ice. Oil spills, like the huge one caused by a tanker accident in Alaska in the spring of 1989, are especially destructive. The plant life, and the animal life that depends on it, have been permanently upset.

This gannet was killed by oil pollution

Fortunately, a lot of the commercial activity in the Arctic and Antarctic is being controlled. The countries responsible for developing the two polar regions have signed various treaties and agreements. There are now international laws that restrict the hunting of many polar animals to certain numbers each year. Other laws limit mineral exploration and building to areas where they will not disrupt the environment, and thus the wildlife, too greatly.

Freeing Gray Whales in Alaska

Identification chart

This chart shows you many of the polar animals described in this book, along with a few others you are likely to read about elsewhere. To see most of them you will have to go to a zoo. Each square of the large grid represents 20 inches and of the small grid 6.5 feet.

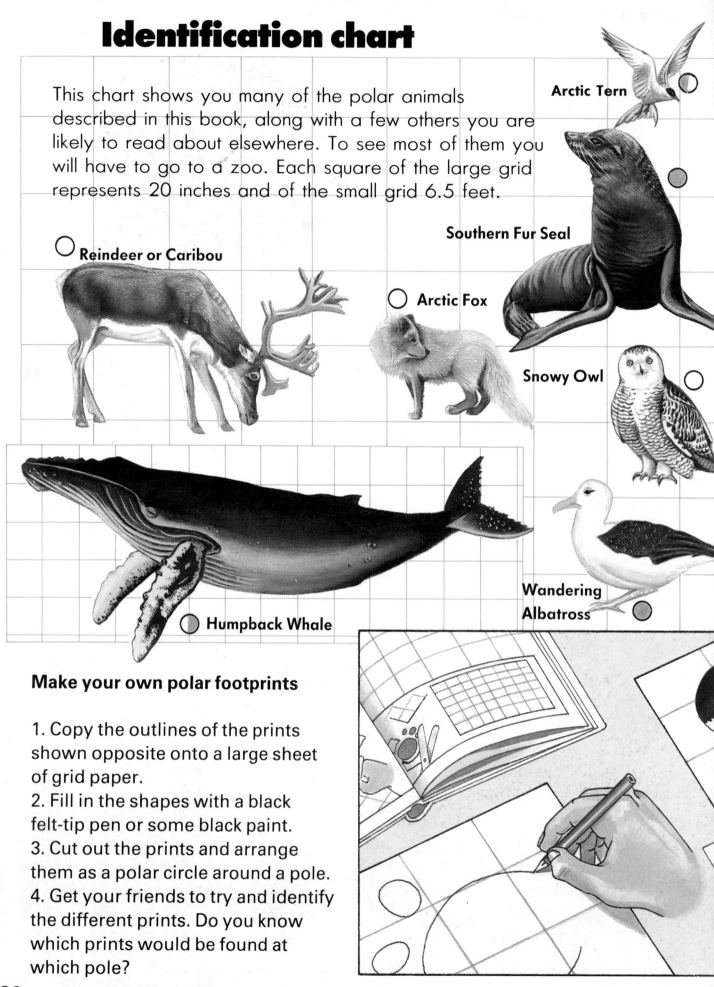

Arctic Tern

Southern Fur Seal

Reindeer or Caribou

Arctic Fox

Snowy Owl

Humpback Whale

Wandering Albatross

Make your own polar footprints

1. Copy the outlines of the prints shown opposite onto a large sheet of grid paper.
2. Fill in the shapes with a black felt-tip pen or some black paint.
3. Cut out the prints and arrange them as a polar circle around a pole.
4. Get your friends to try and identify the different prints. Do you know which prints would be found at which pole?

Antarctic Arctic

Polar Bear

Musk-ox

Arctic Hare

Adelie Penguin

Puffin

Walrus

Emperor Penguin

Penguin   Ermine   Snowshoe Hare

The Pole

Polar Bear

Arctic Fox

Seal

Musk-ox   Goose

99

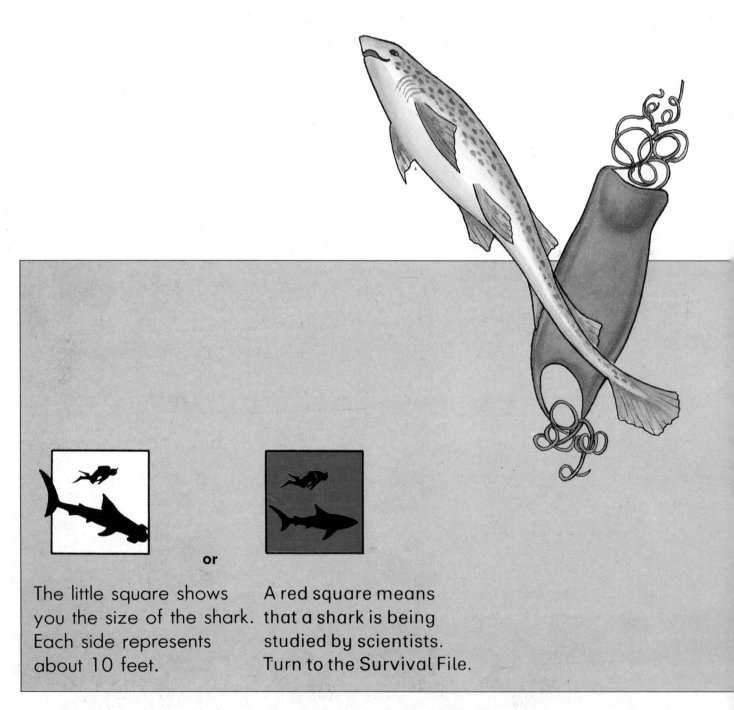

or

The little square shows you the size of the shark. Each side represents about 10 feet.

A red square means that a shark is being studied by scientists. Turn to the Survival File.

The picture opposite is a White-tip Shark photographed in the Red Sea

Chapter 4
SHARKS
Alwyne Wheeler

Facts to Know

There were plenty of sharks in the sea 350 million years ago, long before mammals, birds or other fishes were common. So sharks are survivors of the prehistoric age, ideally suited to the world they live in. There are about 340 different kinds of shark known today. Many of them are magnificent creatures.

Like all other animals, sharks need to be protected — perhaps more so, because so few people like them. In fact, most sharks live far out to sea and are unlikely to attack a human.

Scientists are trying to find out more about sharks. Swimmers might be able to avoid attack if they understand why sharks behave in a certain way.

◁ **Close encounter with a Blue Shark**

Streamlined for speed

Sharks are perfectly built for life in the sea. Their streamlined shape and the way in which the high tail fin is balanced by the pectoral fins means that they can swim and dive effortlessly. Their long tails drive them along at a gentle cruising speed. When hunting they can travel at about 21mph to catch fast-swimming animals such as squids, anchovies and flying fishes.

Many sharks, like the Blue Shark, are powerful long-distance swimmers, too. Blue Sharks are found all around the world where the sea is warm. In summertime they follow the warmer water. Blue Sharks live near the surface. The clear blue of their backs and pure white coloring of the underside are typical of sharks that live near the surface of the sea.

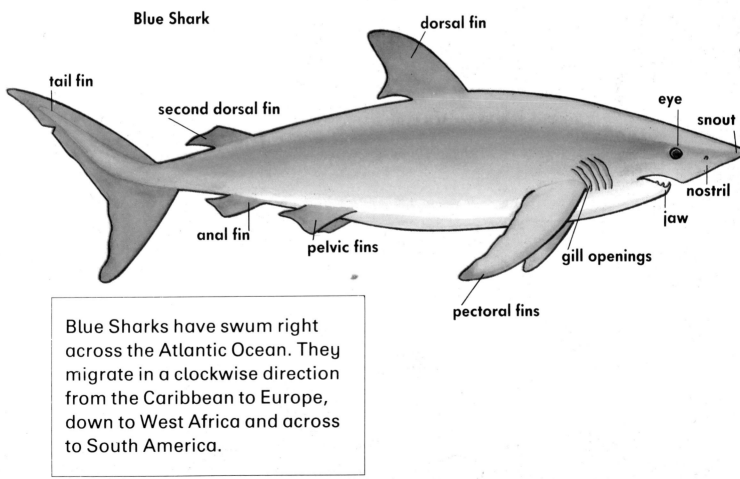

Blue Shark

dorsal fin

tail fin

second dorsal fin

eye

snout

nostril

jaw

anal fin

pelvic fins

gill openings

pectoral fins

Blue Sharks have swum right across the Atlantic Ocean. They migrate in a clockwise direction from the Caribbean to Europe, down to West Africa and across to South America.

◁ **A Blue Shark, perfect swimming machine**

Non-stop swimmers

Active sharks that live near the surface of the sea, like the White-tip Shark, keep moving all their lives. They never stop swimming and go to sleep. Sharks that live on the seabed may lie still for hours on end. Some may find underwater caves in which they can snooze. Unlike most fishes, sharks do not have an air bladder to help them float. Instead they have a large, oily liver which does the same job.

Sharks get a constant supply of oxygen when they swim continuously. A steady stream of water flows over their gills and out of the five gill slits on each side of the head. The gills extract oxygen from the water. If the shark stops swimming or is trapped, the water no longer flows over its gills. Then it cannot take in oxygen and it drowns.

White-tip Shark

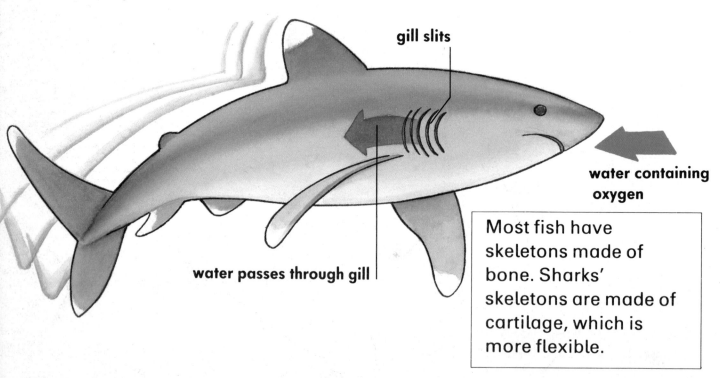

gill slits

water containing oxygen

water passes through gill

Most fish have skeletons made of bone. Sharks' skeletons are made of cartilage, which is more flexible.

The White-tip Shark is probably the most common of the big sharks in the open sea ▷

Extra senses

Sharks depend very heavily on smell to find their food.
Their nostrils are quite large and far apart. When
searching for food sharks swing their heads from side
to side and turn to where they smell the strongest
scent. Scientists think that sharks sometimes bump
an object to "taste" it through taste cells in the skin.
Incredibly sensitive cells on a shark's snout pick up the
tiniest electrical discharges from a nearby animal.
They can also feel vibrations along the sensitive
"lateral line" when an animal is struggling in the
water. On top of all this, they can smell blood in the
water even when it is diluted ten million times. So they
do not depend on their eyesight to hunt their prey.

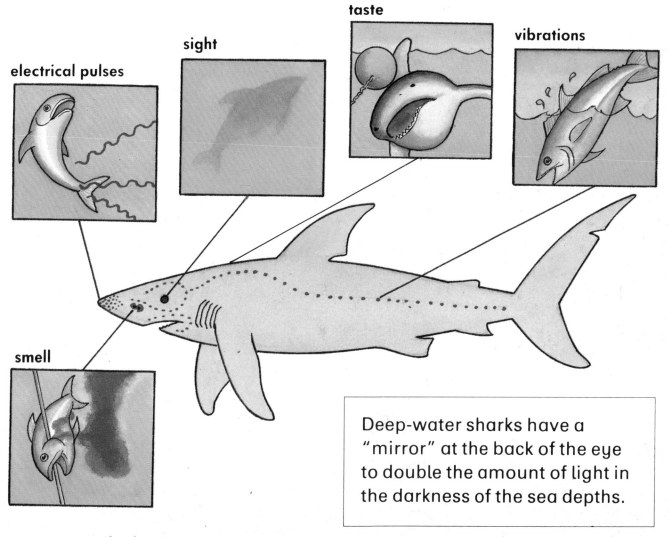

taste

sight

vibrations

electrical pulses

smell

Deep-water sharks have a
"mirror" at the back of the eye
to double the amount of light in
the darkness of the sea depths.

◁ **A Lemon Shark**

Teeth for biting

Sharks never stop growing new teeth. All of them have many rows of teeth in both jaws. As the front ones wear down and fall out they are replaced by new teeth from inside the jaw. The Lemon Shark replaces about 30 teeth each week.

The shape of a shark's teeth depends on the food it eats. The Tiger Shark often eats turtles. It has saw-edged teeth in both jaws. It bites the turtle and then shakes its head slowly from side to side so that the teeth saw through the shell and bones. The Port Jackson Shark has large, flat teeth for crushing sea-urchins, prawns and crabs. The Nurse Shark uses its heavy jaws for crushing shellfish while its hundreds of small, pointed teeth hold the food still.

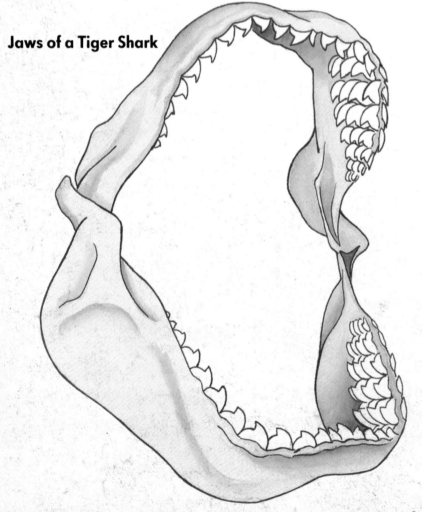

Jaws of a Tiger Shark

The power of a shark's bite is immense—a pressure of 42,600 pounds per square inch compared with a human bite of 142 pounds per square inch.

Lemon

White

Tiger

Port Jackson

Blue

Great Hammerhead

Nurse

A Sand Tiger Shark showing its teeth ▷

Unfussy diet

Most active sharks have sharp-edged or spiky teeth. They feed on many different kinds of prey. Some, like the Blue Shark, eat fast-swimming squids and all kinds of fishes that live in the surface waters. Other sharks, like the Tiger Shark, seem to eat almost anything they come across—dolphins, sea mammals, seabirds and turtles. Fishermen have found old boots, tin cans, beef bones, floats from fishing nets, the head of a sheep and even a dead dog inside Tiger Sharks. Much of this was garbage dumped in the sea. It is easy to see why the Tiger Shark has been called the garbage can of the sea!

When several sharks pick up the scent of blood they rush in to bite at the prey in a "feeding frenzy."

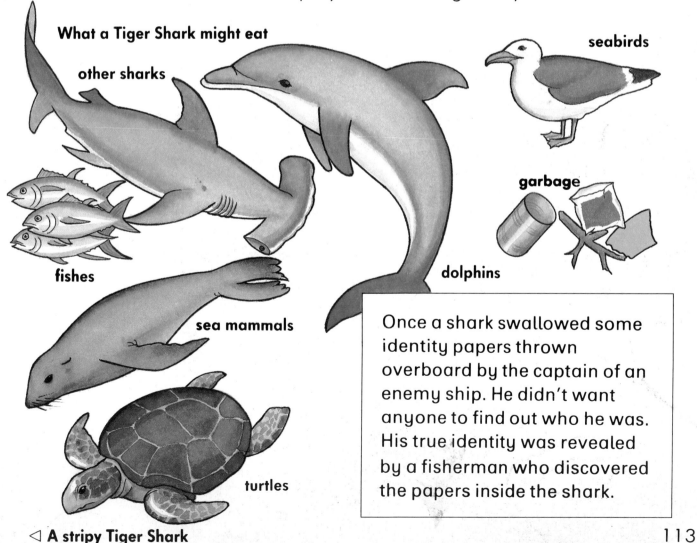

What a Tiger Shark might eat

other sharks

seabirds

garbage

fishes

dolphins

sea mammals

turtles

Once a shark swallowed some identity papers thrown overboard by the captain of an enemy ship. He didn't want anyone to find out who he was. His true identity was revealed by a fisherman who discovered the papers inside the shark.

◁ **A stripy Tiger Shark**

113

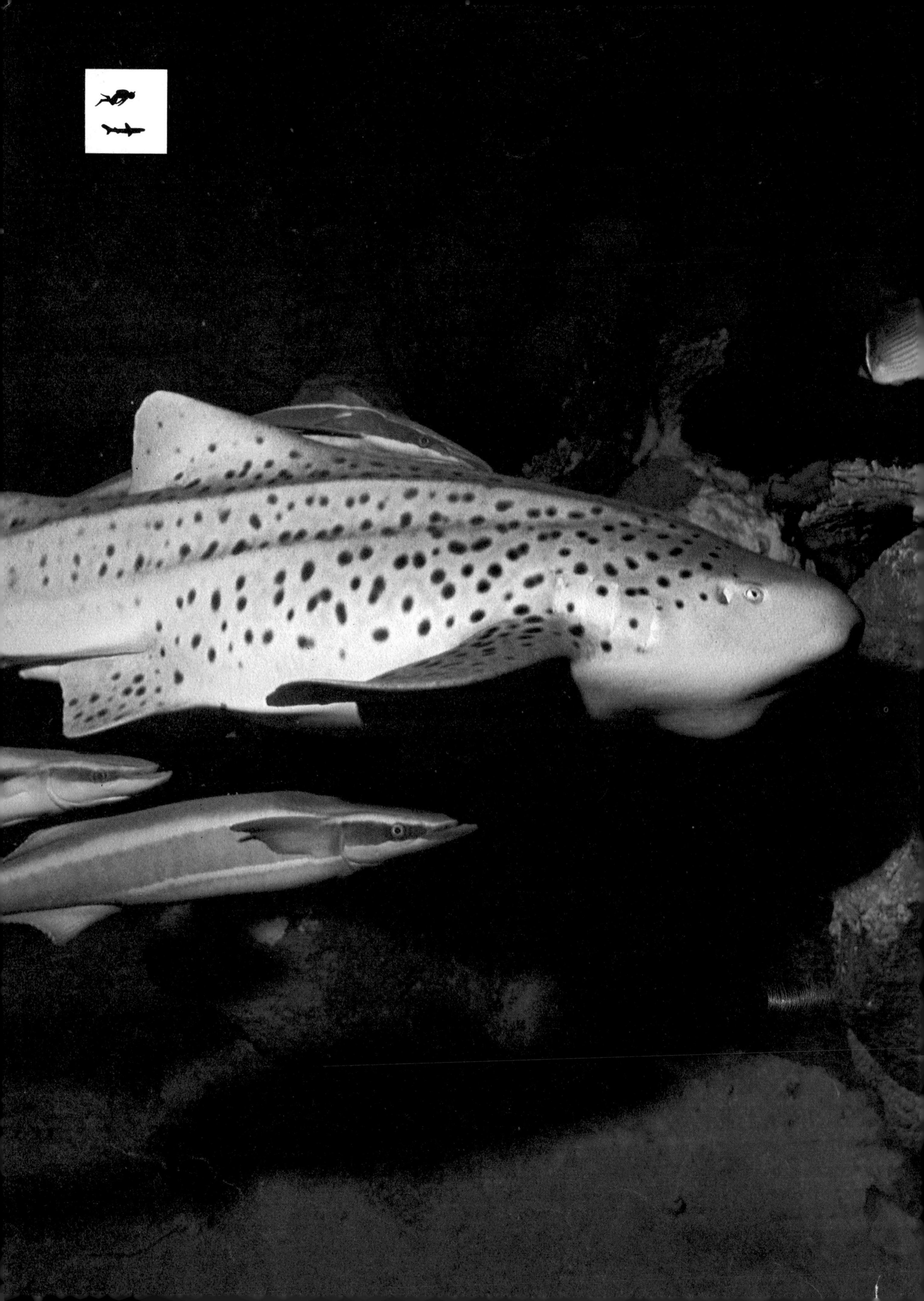

Fellow travelers

Sometimes sharks travel in groups, but often they hunt alone. Even those lone hunters are usually accompanied by smaller fishes, which swim close by. Pilot fishes have dark stripes across their bodies. They hide in the shadow of the shark, protected from their enemies but able to dart out and snap up any suitable food.

Shark suckers and remoras are sucker fish that actually hitch a ride on the shark. They cling to its rough skin by a sucker on top of the head and back. They usually stay close to the shark, feeding on any parasites that attach themselves to it. They also feed on small creatures passing by.

top view of a remora

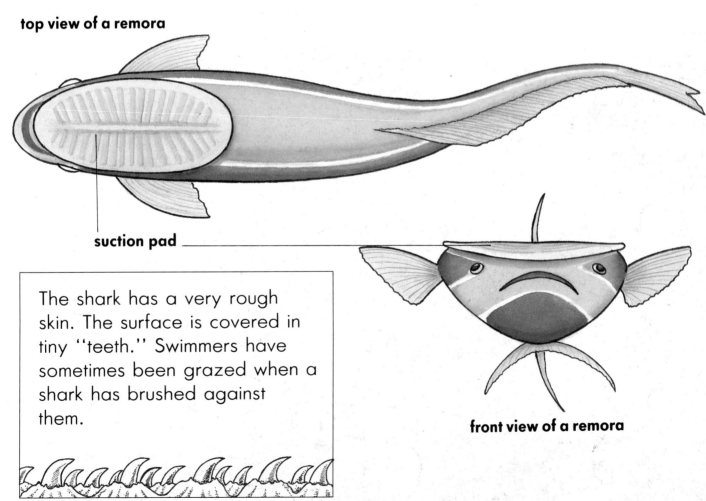

suction pad

The shark has a very rough skin. The surface is covered in tiny "teeth." Swimmers have sometimes been grazed when a shark has brushed against them.

front view of a remora

◁ **A Leopard Shark with shark suckers**

Gentle giants

Three kinds of very large shark are harmless, slow-moving giants. The Whale Shark, the biggest known shark at 45 feet long, lives in tropical seas. It swims along sucking in minute animal plankton. Sometimes it feeds on anchovies, sardines and other small fishes.

Basking Sharks live in cooler, temperate seas and grow up to about 33 feet. They feed on animal plankton by swimming along with their mouths open.

Megamouth has only been found twice. It grows to 15 feet. It lives in deep water and feeds only on deep-sea shrimps. They are attracted by light organs that glow inside its huge mouth.

▽ **A Basking Shark with its mouth open**

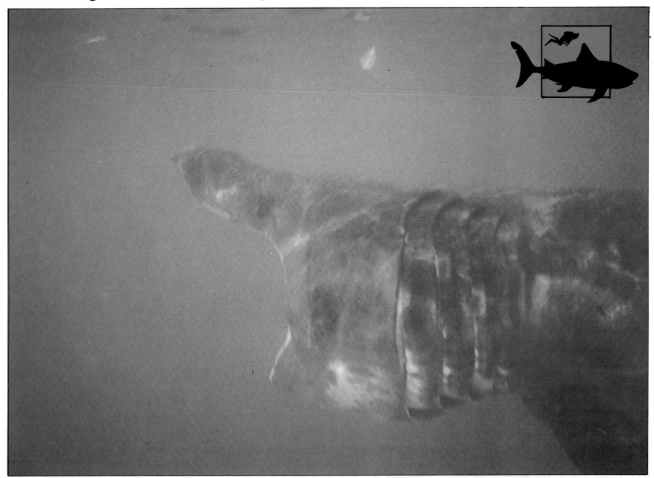

◁ **A Whale Shark**

Unsafe waters

Sometimes swimmers are killed by sharks. Altogether there are around 100 shark attacks on people each year, but only about 25 to 30 of the victims actually die. Almost all attacks take place in the warm waters around the coasts of Australia, South Africa and the warmer coasts of North America. This is partly because the heat seems to make the sharks more aggressive.

Only about 20 kinds of sharks are dangerous. The most dangerous of all is probably the Great White Shark. It grows to at least 21 feet, large enough to eat seals, sea lions, porpoises and big fishes as well as occasional swimmers. Most sharks attack when they are frightened or threatened by a swimmer's approach rather than because they are hungry.

70°F summer only

70°F all year

Sharks are attracted by splashing and struggling. If a shark is nearby, a swimmer should swim away strongly and steadily and try not to panic.

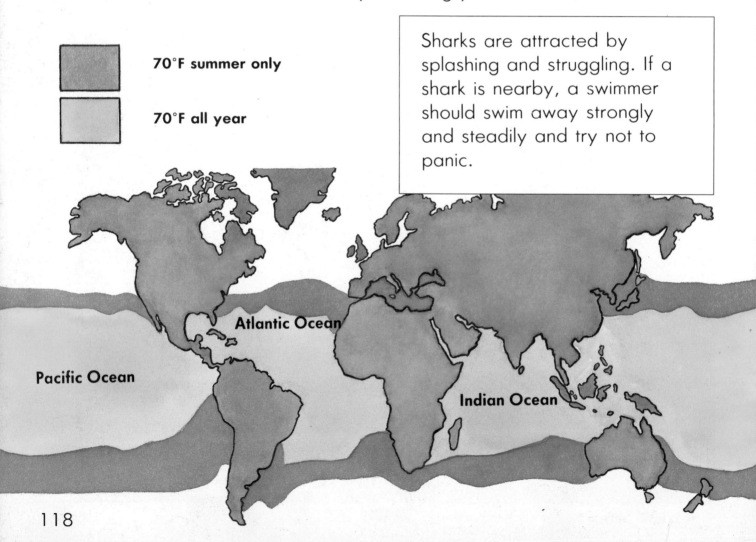

Pacific Ocean

Atlantic Ocean

Indian Ocean

Strange sharks

Hammerhead Sharks have flat heads that extend sideways to form a hammer shape. They have an enormous advantage over other sharks. The eyes at the extreme ends of the hammer are able to see all around the shark, and their widely spaced nostrils help them smell food at a great distance. Hammerheads are usually the first sharks to arrive at a bait.

The Wobbegong lives on the coasts of nothern Australia and Papua New Guinea, usually close to coral reefs. Its mottled coloring and long, fringed beard around its head help it to hide among seaweeds and coral. It lies in wait for fishes, crabs, lobsters or octopuses to come close enough to catch.

▽ **A Wobbegong Shark lying near the seabed**

◁ **The strange Hammerhead Shark**

Shark babies

Most fishes lay their eggs in the water, but sharks do not just abandon their eggs. Many shark babies are kept inside the mother's body until they are big enough to swim and feed on their own. The Blue Shark sometimes has as many as 50 babies at a time, but others, like the Porbeagle, have only one or two. A Spurdog carries her 20 babies inside her for nearly two years before they are born.

The Dogfish—a small shark—lays its eggs in small leathery cases. They have long threads at the corners to tangle in seaweed and stop them from being washed away. The baby Dogfish hatches out after many months when it is about 4 inches in length.

A Dogfish egg is often called a "mermaid's purse"

Dogfish

Shark babies can look after themselves as soon as they are born. They don't stay close to the mother. She takes no further interest in them.

A young Port Jackson Shark ▷

Sharks' enemies

Because many sharks are large and can swim quickly there are very few animals that attack them. Some small or newborn sharks are eaten by bigger sharks, and some are attacked by Orca Whales, Sperm Whales and large fishes. A number of dolphins will attack a shark together to protect their own young. Swordfish have also been known to stab at sharks.

The biggest enemy of sharks is man. About 30 people a year are killed by sharks, but about 4.5 million sharks are killed by people. In some countries sharks like the Dogfish and the Spurdog are used for food.

Dolphins sometimes attack sharks

Shark meat is eaten all over the world. Small sharks sold in fish shops are usually called "flake" or "rock-eel".

125

Survival file

Sharks have survived for millions of years. But even though their ocean habitat is not in any particular danger, they are at risk from the activities of humans who see them as an evil menace. Luckily, there are scientists who want to study sharks and find out more about them. The best place to watch sharks is in their natural surroundings. Divers sometimes stay inside a cage so they cannot be attacked. Then they can film the sharks at close quarters in safety. They attract the sharks with a bait of fresh fish.

Filming a Great White Shark from a cage

Experienced divers sometimes swim freely among the sharks. They carry a stick with an explosive head on it to stave off the dangerous sharks. They try to understand the sharks' "body language." The way a shark moves when it is swimming towards a diver may tell us whether it is aggressive, frightened, curious, hungry or even playful. Divers "tag" sharks by fastening a number onto a fin. If one is recaptured they can see how it has grown and how far it has travelled.

Diver alongside a Whale Shark

Valerie Taylor testing her shark-suit

Scientists can also learn from sharks kept in captivity. They are studying how they hear, how well they can see, and how much they depend on their sense of smell. They want to find out how the organs that detect faint electric discharges from other animals work. It is important to learn about their sense of taste. If scientists can find a substance that sharks do not like, then swimmers and divers will be able to carry it with them in case of attack.

Some naturalists, like the Taylors, find sharks so fascinating that they have made them a lifetime's study.

Identification chart

This chart shows you some of the more common sharks. You can see some of them in the zoo. The sharks are drawn to scale to show their comparative sizes. The sides of each square of the grid represent one foot.

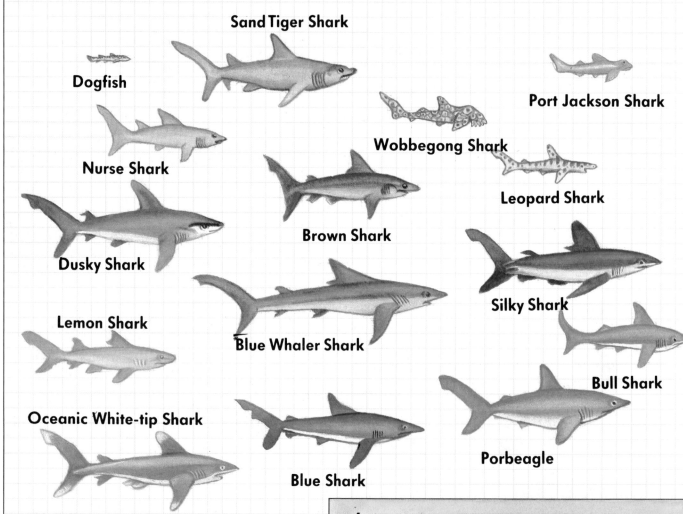

Dogfish

Sand Tiger Shark

Port Jackson Shark

Nurse Shark

Wobbegong Shark

Leopard Shark

Brown Shark

Dusky Shark

Silky Shark

Lemon Shark

Blue Whaler Shark

Bull Shark

Oceanic White-tip Shark

Blue Shark

Porbeagle

Draw a life-size shark

1. Make yourself a huge sheet of paper.
2. Divide it into (roughly) one-foot squares.
3. Copy your shark from these pages, using the squares here to help you.
4. Color in your shark.
5. Cut it out carefully.
6. You can mount it on stiff paper.

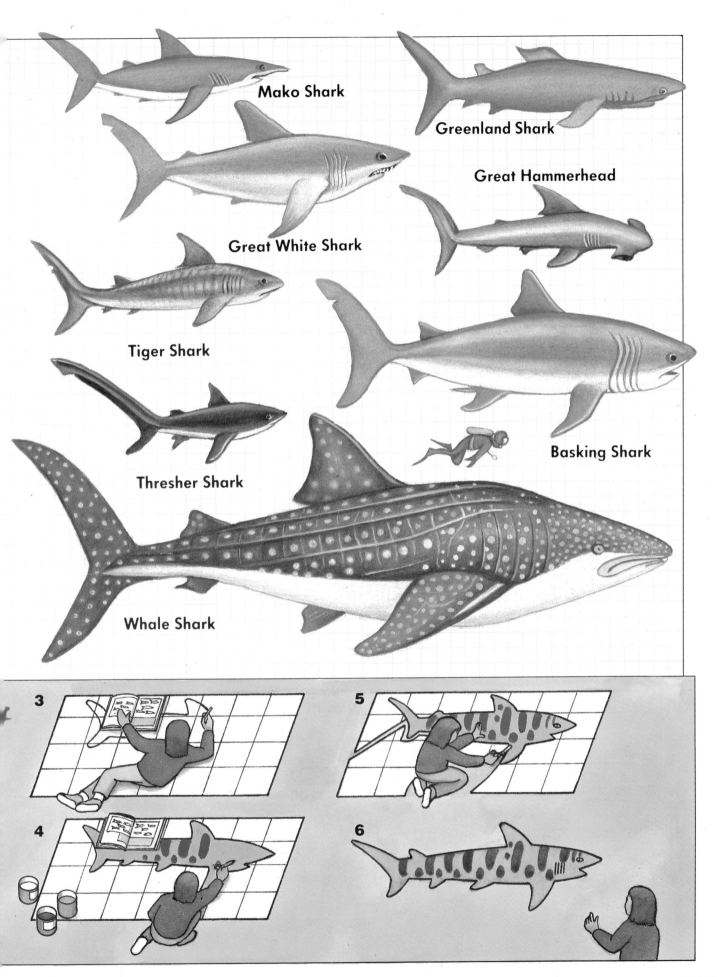

Mako Shark

Greenland Shark

Great Hammerhead

Great White Shark

Tiger Shark

Basking Shark

Thresher Shark

Whale Shark

3

4

5

6

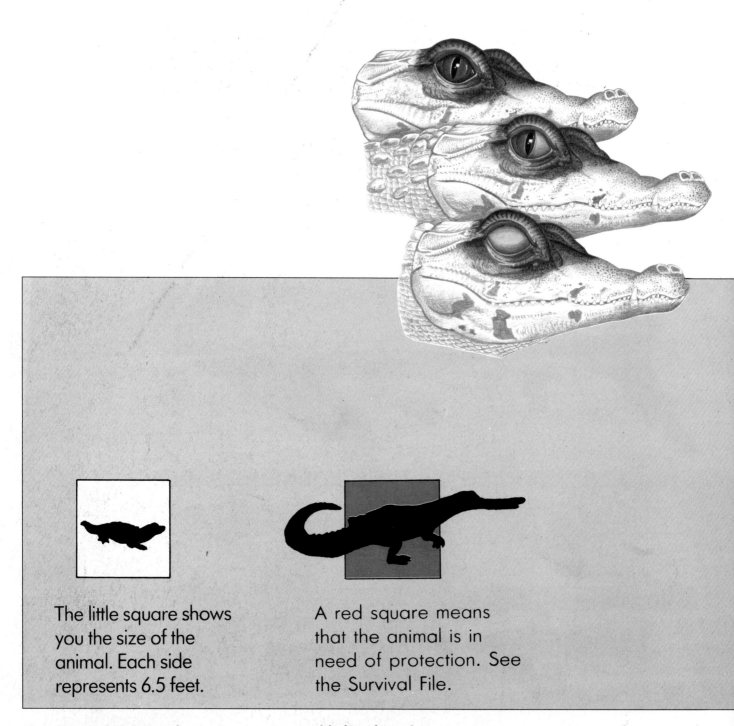

The little square shows you the size of the animal. Each side represents 6.5 feet.

A red square means that the animal is in need of protection. See the Survival File.

The picture opposite shows a young crocodile hatching from its egg

Chapter 5
CROCODILES AND ALLIGATORS

Lionel Bender

Facts to Know

Crocodiles and alligators are the only survivors of a group of reptiles that dominated the Earth about 200 to 65 million years ago, a group that included the dinosaurs. The crocodile and alligator family consists of 22 species of reptiles that are adapted for life in and around water. The family includes the true crocodiles, which live in Africa, Asia and Australia, the alligators of North and South America and China, the caimans of South America, and the Gharial, or Gavial, of India. Together they are known as crocodilians.

Crocodiles and alligators are most common in hot tropical regions, but they also live in areas where there are warm summers and cool winters. They are all hunters and they feed on animals that range from deer and cattle to fish and birds.

◁ **An American Alligator stretches out of the water to catch a young Egret**

◁ **A crocodile basks in the sun on a riverbank**

midday

Most crocodiles keep their bodies at 85-97°F. This is a few degrees cooler than ours. They become sluggish at below 68°F.

morning

evening

When the sun gets too hot, the crocodile slinks into the water.

A crocodile warms up by basking in the morning sun.

It warms up again in late afternoon and early evening.

Cold-blooded

Crocodiles and alligators, like other reptiles, are cold-blooded. This means they cannot adjust their body temperature by producing body heat, as we can. They have to rely on their surroundings to keep their bodies warm enough to work properly. This is why they are most common in warm countries.

When they are active, or as they bask in the sun, their temperature rises. Crocodiles and alligators usually lie with their mouths open when they are too hot. This helps them lose heat. They cannot sweat to cool down. But when their temperature increases to well above normal, they must stop moving, rest in the shade, or slink into the water.

135

Life in water

Crocodilians are difficult to see when they lie in the water. They are often mistaken for logs. Their eyes and nostrils are set high on their heads. This means that they can see and breathe when they are floating almost totally underwater. They use sideways sweeps of their large, powerful, flattened tails to swim along. When danger threatens, they sink quickly downwards and backwards using a sudden upward movement of their webbed hind feet.

Underwater, crocodilians keep their nostrils and ears closed. A special flap of skin sweeps sideways across each eye to give protection during diving. The animals can hold their breath for more than an hour.

A Gharial swimming in a river, showing the sideways motion of its tail

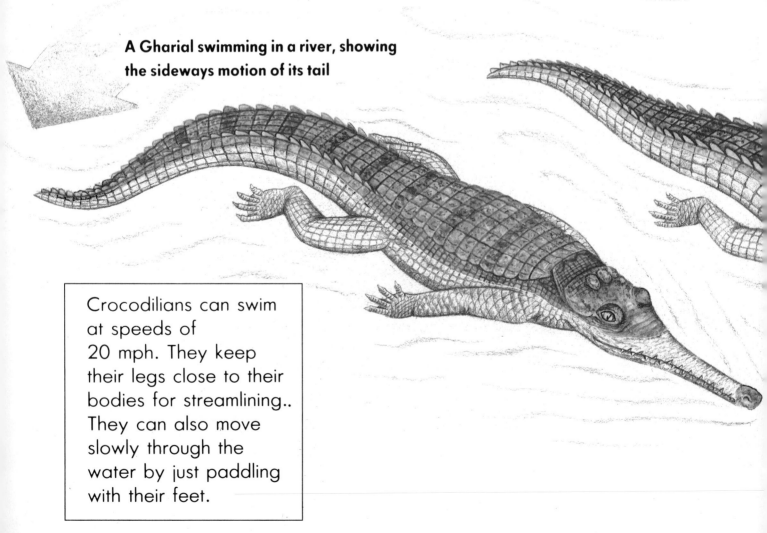

Crocodilians can swim at speeds of 20 mph. They keep their legs close to their bodies for streamlining.. They can also move slowly through the water by just paddling with their feet.

An American Alligator cruises through the water

137

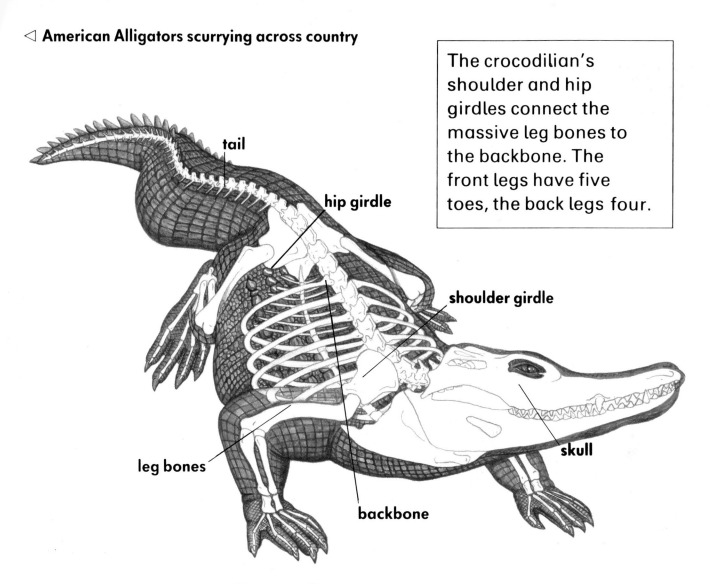

tail

hip girdle

The crocodilian's shoulder and hip girdles connect the massive leg bones to the backbone. The front legs have five toes, the back legs four.

shoulder girdle

leg bones

skull

backbone

Out on land

The Australian Freshwater Crocodile and the Nile Crocodile can gallop across country, with front and back legs working together like a bounding squirrel. But usually crocodiles walk on dry land by stretching their legs and lifting their bodies well off the ground. Alligators and caimans usually slink about, moving slowly forward on their stomachs with their legs spread out to either side.

The Gharial and the Saltwater Crocodile of Southeast Asia rarely move more than a few yards from their river and estuary homes. But species that live in ponds and lakes, such as the Indian Marsh Crocodile, may travel many miles overland in search of water if their homes dry up.

Big and small

Crocodiles and alligators grow rapidly in areas where they can find plenty of food and it is warm all year round. The biggest crocodilian on record was an Estuarine Crocodile from Bengal that is thought to have measured 33 feet in length and weighted more than two tons. The Smooth-fronted Caiman and African Dwarf Crocodile, on the other hand, barely reach 5 feet as adults.

Crocodilians continue to grow throughout their lives, and they can live for many years—American Alligators may live for up to 70 years. This means that several species can grow very large. But today poachers kill the largest specimens and so individuals over 20 feet long are rare.

A Dwarf Caiman looks for a meal with only its head out of the water

The Estuarine Crocodile, like all crocodilians, continues to grow throughout its life ▷

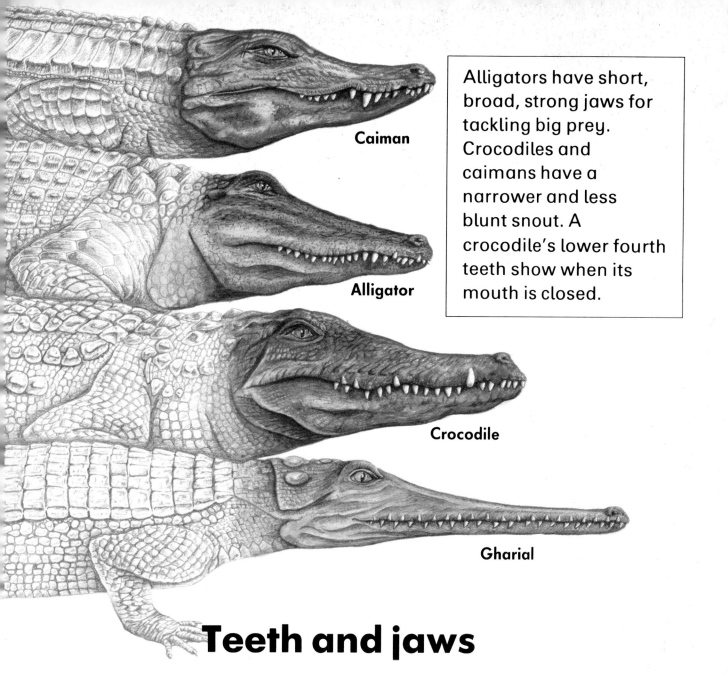

Caiman

Alligator

Crocodile

Gharial

Alligators have short, broad, strong jaws for tackling big prey. Crocodiles and caimans have a narrower and less blunt snout. A crocodile's lower fourth teeth show when its mouth is closed.

Teeth and jaws

The Gharial is a fish-eater that has about 160 teeth. These are small and pointed so that the animal can keep hold of its slippery prey. Crocodiles and alligators have about 100 teeth. Their teeth are good for holding flesh, but not for cutting or chewing it. Crocodiles hold food in their teeth and thrash it about to tear it apart. They can then swallow the food in large chunks.

Crocodiles and alligators often lose teeth in struggles with large prey. But the teeth are quickly replaced. Each tooth contains a small replacement tooth inside it. A crocodilian may produce fifty or more sets of teeth within its lifetime.

◁ **A Gharial with its bulb-like nose**

143

Hunting and feeding

Fish, birds, snakes, lizards, frogs, turtles, rats, deer, zebra and cattle are all part of the diet of crocodiles, alligators and caimans. As babies, however, crocodilians eat mainly insects, frogs and small fish. The Gharial eats nothing but fish.

The American Alligator often captures prey by lying in wait in shallow water or within pools along the riverbank. As a victim approaches, the alligator seizes it, drags it underwater and then tears it apart. Crocodiles sometimes attack and eat one another. They will even eat people. But this only happens when they cannot find their normal prey. Crocodilians also feed on dead animals—they are both scavengers and hunters.

A young crocodile grips a fish in its pointed teeth

A Nile Crocodile eats a zebra killed by another hunter ▷

Attack and defense

A crocodilian's most effective weapons are its powerful jaws. Once these are closed tight, no animal can escape their grip. A crocodilian will sometimes use its tail to knock over an animal before trying to eat it. Male alligators fight over females at mating time, tearing at each other with their teeth.

Despite their fierceness, crocodiles and alligators do have enemies. Crocodiles may be killed in fights with lions and leopards. A mother elephant or hippo will also attack a crocodile that threatens her young. But most crocodilians are so well camouflaged in drab greens and browns that they usually surprise and then easily overpower their prey.

Male alligators will often attack one another fiercely

146   **An American Alligator, covered with and surrounded by algae, waits for a meal ▷**

Senses and sounds

Vision and hearing are crocodilians' most important senses. They rely mainly on vision to hunt and capture prey. When their ears are out of the water, they can hear well, too. They keep in touch with one another using a variety of sounds. Baby crocodiles peep loudly when they hatch from their eggs so that their mother will help them out of the nest. Male and female crocodilians roar and croak loudly at each other at mating time.

Crocodiles and alligators swallow their food underwater in large chunks and so they do not need good senses of smell and taste. Their skin is thick and leathery and not very sensitive to touch.

Crocodiles and alligators possess a third eyelid that moves sideways across the eye.

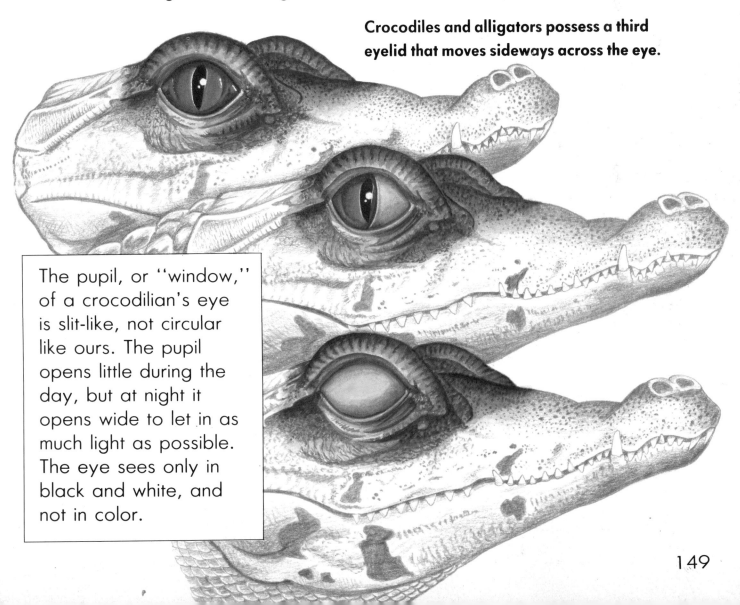

The pupil, or "window," of a crocodilian's eye is slit-like, not circular like ours. The pupil opens little during the day, but at night it opens wide to let in as much light as possible. The eye sees only in black and white, and not in color.

Courtship and mating

At mating time, the male crocodilian courts the female. An adult male Gharial has a swelling on its snout that probably helps to attract a mate. A male Nile Crocodile displays his desire to mate by thrashing about in the water and keeping his mouth open. He comes alongside the female in the water and puts his legs on her back. The pair then sink to the bottom of the river or lake and mate.

About two months after mating, the female is ready to lay her eggs. While she is pregnant she prepares a nest, which acts as an incubator to protect the eggs and keep them warm. The male rarely helps in nest building, or in looking after the eggs.

A male Gharial (left) approaches a female as a plover looks on

A female Estuarine Crocodile guards her nest ▷

An alligator's egg showing the developing embryo within the fluid-filled sac

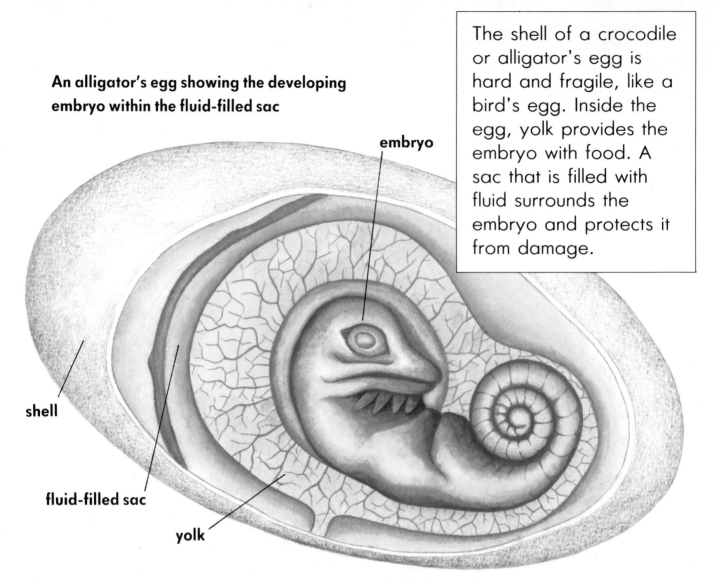

embryo

The shell of a crocodile or alligator's egg is hard and fragile, like a bird's egg. Inside the egg, yolk provides the embryo with food. A sac that is filled with fluid surrounds the embryo and protects it from damage.

shell

fluid-filled sac

yolk

Eggs and hatchlings

A female alligator or female Gharial lays between 15 and 80 eggs. A female Nile Crocodile lays as many as 90, each the size of a goose egg. The Gharial digs out a hollow in the ground for a nest. Alligators make a heap of water plants, lay the eggs on the top, then cover them with more plant material. Crocodiles often just bury their eggs in the sand.

The baby crocodilians hatch between nine and 17 weeks later. Sometimes the mother picks up eggs that have not hatched and gently crushes them in her jaws to free the young. Hatchlings look like small versions of their parents. Even those of the 20 foot-long Nile Crocodile are less than 12 inches in length.

Young crocodilians often hatch within moments of each other ▷

Growing up

Newborn crocodiles and alligators cannot look after themselves very well. Many are eaten by fish, birds, mammals and other reptiles, especially large lizards such as monitors. However, their mothers usually protect them for the first few months. Nile and Estuarine Crocodile mothers often carry their young from the nest to the water in their mouths. A mother Gharial will carry her young on her back.

The young grow quickly, almost doubling their length in the first year. The American Alligator grows 10 to 12 inches each year. It is adult when it is five years old. Most crocodilians are ready to mate by the time they are eight years old.

A young alligator hitches a ride on its mother's back

A young crocodile about to devour a crab ▷

Survival file

In many parts of Africa, South America, Australia and India, the native people kill alligators and crocodiles for food. This hunting has been going on for hundreds of years. But because these people only kill as many animals as they need, they do not threaten the survival of crocodilians. Since the 1950s, however, commercial hunters have killed crocodilians in the tens of thousands just for their skins. The skins are used to make handbags, shoes and wallets, which are sold in shops all over the world.

In a nature reserve, crocodiles are given water buffalo to eat

Crocodiles and alligators are now also threatened by local farmers, who destroy their homes. The farmers drain lakes, ponds and swamps for land on which to graze their animals or grow crops. In India, hunting and habitat destruction reduced the number of Gharials in the wild to less than 100 in 1974.

Since about 1975, there has been a worldwide ban on trade in the skins of most crocodiles and alligators. But illegal hunting and egg-collecting still go on. There is also a growing trade in capturing crocodilians to be shown in wildlife parks and kept as pets. Most of those sold as pets are killed once they get too big.

Trade in crocodilian skins continues

Rangers sometimes have to kill alligators

In India, Australia and America, there are now crocodile and alligator farms that are helping to increase the numbers of crocodilians in the wild. Eggs are taken from the wild and kept safely in incubators. The hatchlings are looked after and fed until they are big and strong enough to be released back into the wild. The young are taken to rivers and lakes around the world.

Identification chart

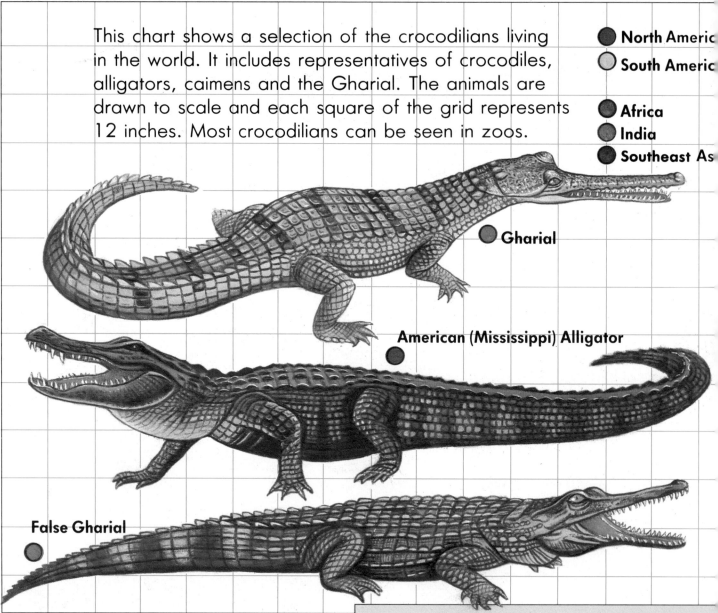

This chart shows a selection of the crocodilians living in the world. It includes representatives of crocodiles, alligators, caimens and the Gharial. The animals are drawn to scale and each square of the grid represents 12 inches. Most crocodilians can be seen in zoos.

● North Americ
○ South Americ
● Africa
◐ India
● Southeast As

● Gharial

American (Mississippi) Alligator

False Gharial

Make Crocodilian Snap

1. Trace the heads of the four types of crocodilian shown on these pages onto pieces of cardboard.

2. Make about six of each type of playing card.

3. Use the cards to play Snap or Pairs, matching the shapes of the heads and tooth patterns.

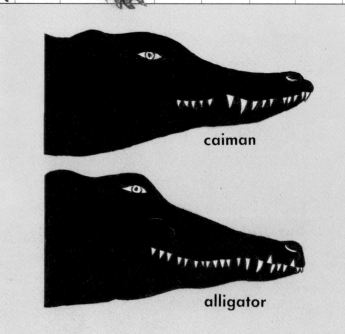

caiman

alligator

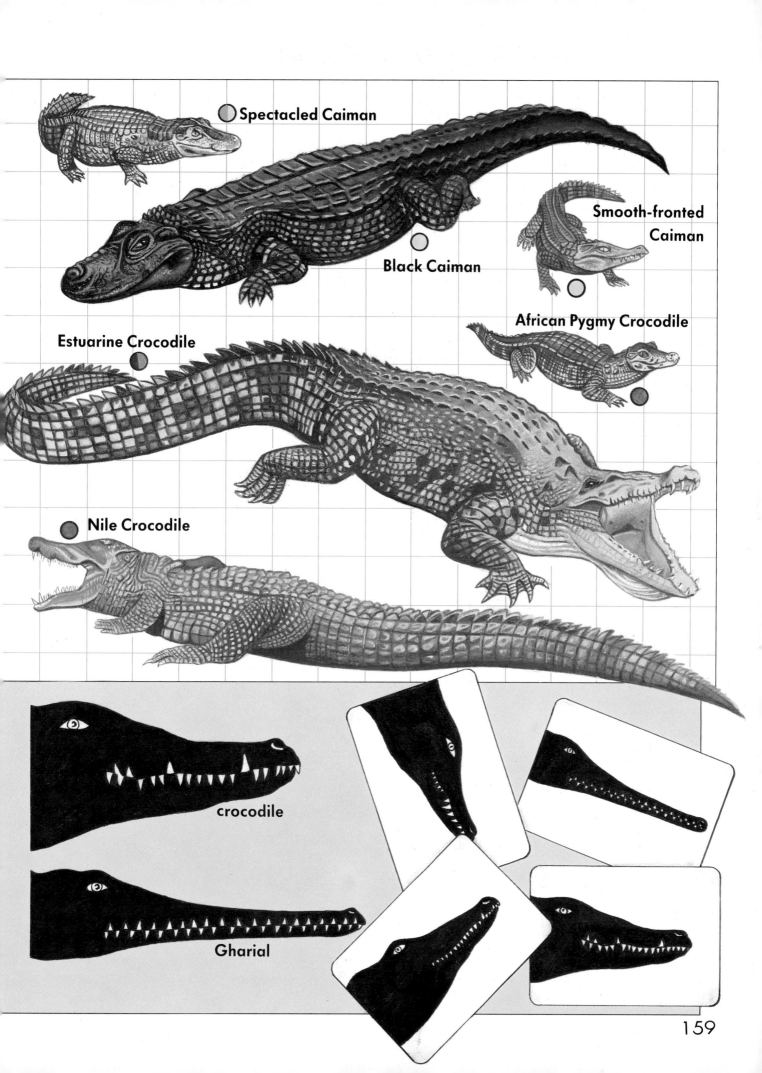

Spectacled Caiman

Black Caiman

Smooth-fronted Caiman

African Pygmy Crocodile

Estuarine Crocodile

Nile Crocodile

crocodile

Gharial

159

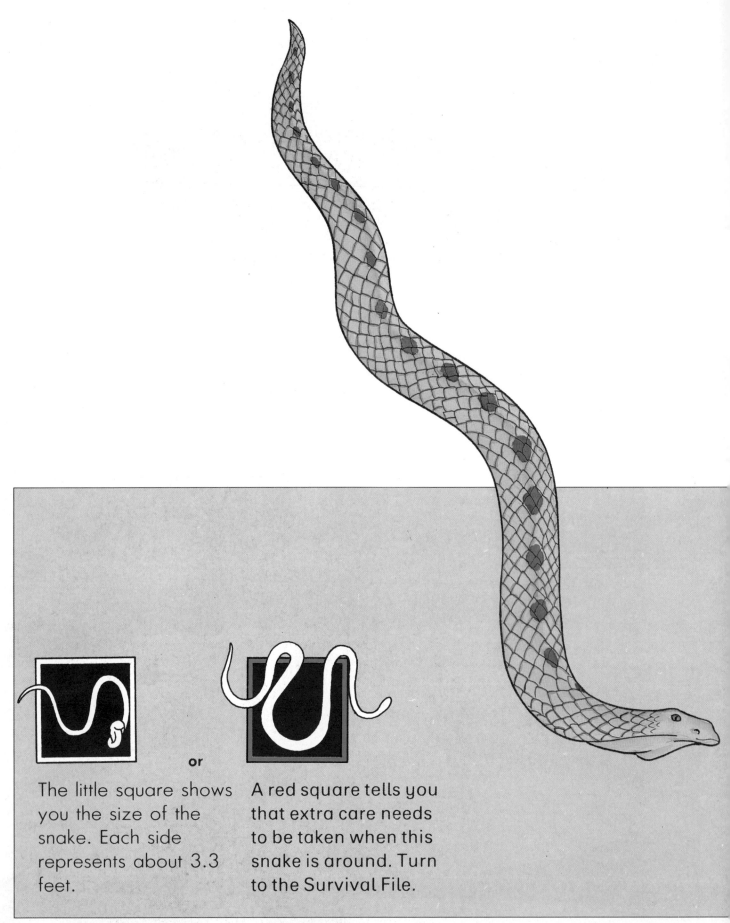

The little square shows you the size of the snake. Each side represents about 3.3 feet.

or

A red square tells you that extra care needs to be taken when this snake is around. Turn to the Survival File.

The picture opposite shows a Puff Adder with its young

160

Chapter 6
POISONOUS SNAKES
Colin McCarthy

Facts to Know

Poisonous snakes use poison to kill their prey. Other snakes are constrictors, which coil themselves around their victims to kill them. A few very dangerous poisonous snakes do kill people, but most snakes are not harmful to humans and there is no need to fear them.

Even dangerous snakes are fascinating animals, which bring benefits as well as harm. In some places they keep down rodents and other pests. Scientists are learning more about human nerves and blood by studying the snake venoms that attack them.

It is best to treat all snakes with respect and to take extra care when walking in places where snakes live.

◁ **Puff Adders are hard to see when they lie still**

How poisonous?

A poisonous snake uses its venom to kill its prey. If it has caught a rat or a bird, it injects the right amount of venom to kill an animal of that size.

Even newly hatched snakes emerge ready to catch food for themselves. These tiny poisonous snakes arrive with enough venom to kill four mice.

The King Cobra is the longest poisonous snake of all. It can grow up to 16.5 feet. It feeds on other snakes, but it is particularly dangerous to humans because it can inject large quantities of venom when it chooses. The Indian Cobra is smaller but it bites more people because it is found near villages.

**Baby snakes emerging from their shells
ready to take care of themselves**

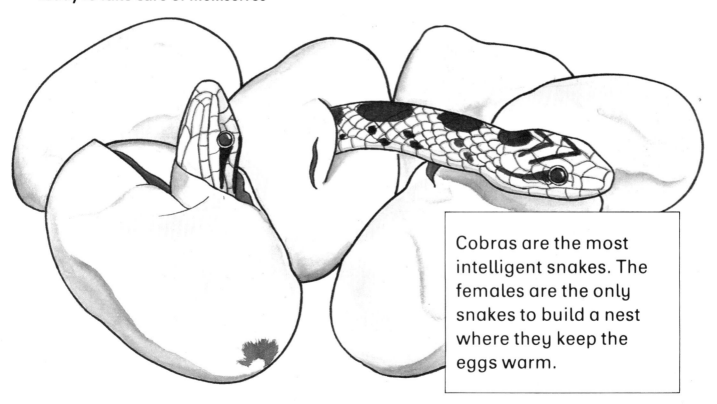

Cobras are the most intelligent snakes. The females are the only snakes to build a nest where they keep the eggs warm.

◁ **The King Cobra rears up when alarmed**

Venom

Venom is the mixture of poisonous substances that these snakes use to kill their prey. It is produced in special glands that lie between the snake's eye and the corner of its mouth. Some of the poisons work on the victim's blood. Others attack its nerves and heart. The venom kills the prey, or at least stops it from moving. It also makes it easier for the snake to digest.

Venom is injected through the snake's fangs. Back-fanged snakes have short, grooved fangs at the back of the upper jaw. In vipers and cobras the venom flows through hollow fangs at the front of the mouth. Cobras have "fixed" front fangs. Vipers have longer front fangs that fold in when not in use.

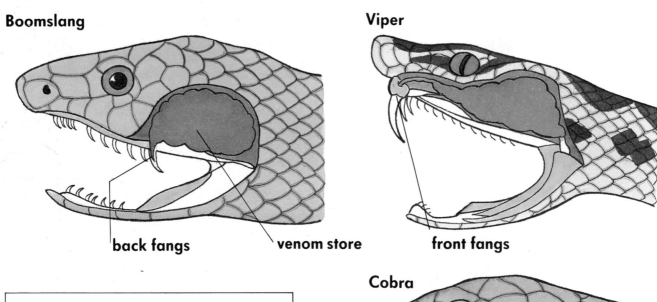

Boomslang

back fangs   venom store

Viper

front fangs

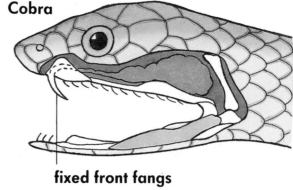

Cobra

fixed front fangs

A spitting cobra makes spectacular use of its venom to defend itself. It sprays jets of venom from its fangs into the eyes of an enemy. The victim can be blinded if not treated right away.

Black-necked Spitting Cobra spraying venom ▷

A bite to eat

Once a snake has a good grip on its victim it swallows it whole, even though the prey sometimes looks impossibly large. This is because the lower jaws are connected to the skull by hinge-like bones that allow the snake to open its mouth very wide. The ligament stretching between each side of the lower jaw is also very elastic. It can sometimes take a snake about an hour to swallow a large animal.

The European Adder below feeds on small mammals and frogs. It is a small viper that is found all over Europe, even in cold places. Its bite is not usually serious to humans. The Horned Adder is a desert snake that feeds on small mammals and lizards. It moves sideways across the sand.

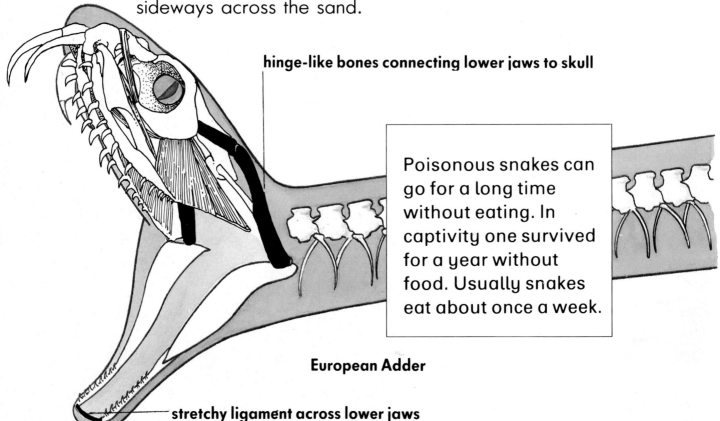

hinge-like bones connecting lower jaws to skull

Poisonous snakes can go for a long time without eating. In captivity one survived for a year without food. Usually snakes eat about once a week.

European Adder

stretchy ligament across lower jaws

A Horned Adder from Namibia swallowing a mouse ▷

Back-fanged snakes

Most back-fanged snakes are completely harmless to humans. Their venom isn't powerful and their fangs are too short to pierce the skin. They need to get a good grip and then chew on their prey to inject the venom. The produce only a small amount of poison.

The Boomslang, a back-fanged tree snake from Africa, is an exception. It is highly poisonous and has been known to kill people, although it usually hunts birds.

The Malayan Golden Tree Snake, also back-fanged, is a "flying snake." Flying snakes can glide from tree to tree. They spread their ribs to make a curved surface that gives them lift, like the wings of an airplane.

The Malayan Golden Tree Snake is not harmful to humans

A famous snake specialist, Karl P. Schmidt, was killed in 1957 when a Boomslang bit him. Up until then it had been considered relatively harmless.

◁ **Boomslang eating a bird**

Cobras and their relatives

Snakes with fixed front fangs – cobras and their relatives – live in warm parts of the world. Cobras rear up when they are alarmed. They spread the loose skin on their necks into a hood. Any bite from a member of the cobra family can be serious.

Kraits and Mambas are cobra relatives. Kraits live in Asia. They are mainly active at night and feed on other snakes. Mambas live in Africa. The highly poisonous Taipans and Tiger Snakes are cobra relatives found in Australia.

Mambas live mostly in trees, but the much-feared Black Mamba is often found on the ground. Mambas are the fastest snakes in the world. They can move at 9 mph, as fast as a ten-year-old sprinter.

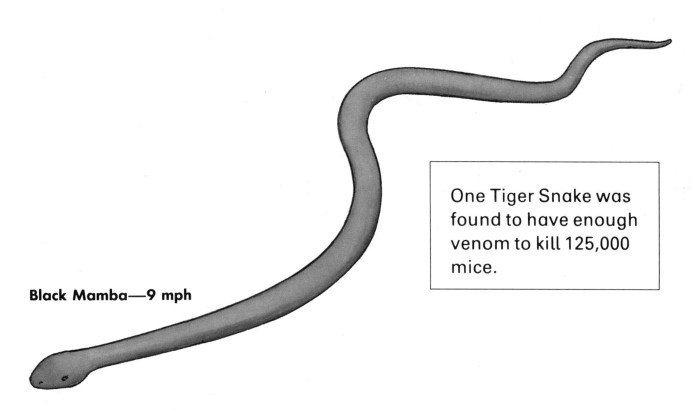

Black Mamba—9 mph

One Tiger Snake was found to have enough venom to kill 125,000 mice.

◁ **A Black Mamba on the ground**

This little rhyme tells American children the difference between a coral snake and a harmless mimic: Red touch yellow, bad for a fellow; Red touch black, good for Jack.

Coral Snake from America

Scarlet King Snake

Warning signals

The colorful coral snakes are the only cobra relatives in the Americas. They also live in Africa and Asia. They usually have a very clear pattern of yellow, black and red bands, which makes them easily seen. The pattern is a warning signal that the snake is dangerous and best left alone. Coral snakes are very poisonous. Many of their victims are young children who pick them up because they are so pretty and seem quite docile.

There are other less harmful snakes that look like coral snakes. They fool their enemies into thinking they are dangerous, so they keep away.

175

Vipers

There are about 170 species of viper. They live in almost all the countries of the world apart from Australia. Vipers have wide, triangular-shaped heads. They have a very efficient way of injecting venom into their prey. When a viper attacks a mouse, for example, it opens its mouth wide, swings its fangs into the upright position and strikes with great speed. As soon as the venom has been injected, the viper releases the mouse. The mouse is not killed immediately and often crawls away. The viper soon tracks it down by its scent. Adders are vipers. The Puff Adder and the Gaboon Viper are both found in Africa.

Puff Adder striking at mouse

The Gaboon Viper has the longest fangs of any snake. They can measure up to 2 inches.

Snake senses

Most snakes have poor sight and not very good hearing. Their sense of smell, though, is excellent. The organs that detect smell are on the roof of a snake's mouth. Scent particles are transferred there by the snake's flicking tongue. Some snakes, called pit vipers, can also sense the body heat of their prey through special heat receptors, or "pits." They can be seen midway between the nostrils and the eyes. These pits are sensitive to any warm object. The snake can strike accurately at its prey, even in the dark.

One of the most deadly pit vipers is the Bushmaster from South America. Luckily it is shy and rarely seen.

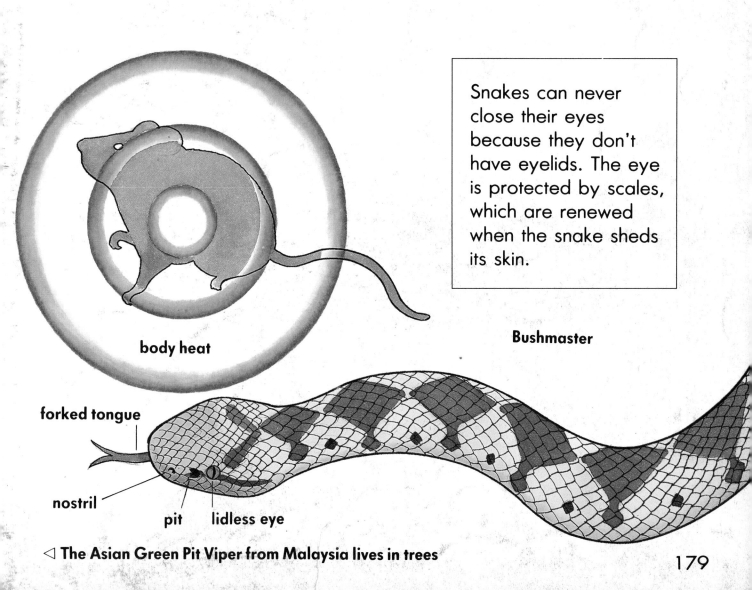

body heat

Snakes can never close their eyes because they don't have eyelids. The eye is protected by scales, which are renewed when the snake sheds its skin.

Bushmaster

forked tongue

nostril

pit   lidless eye

◁ **The Asian Green Pit Viper from Malaysia lives in trees**

Rattlesnakes

Rattlesnakes are pit vipers. There are about 30 species of them living in America. The most remarkable thing about these snakes is the rattle on the end of the tail. A rattlesnake waves its tail when it is alarmed. It makes a whirring, crackling noise when it is shaken. The sound of the rattle warns any animal that might try to attack the snake or accidentally tread on it.

Diamondback rattlesnakes are the most deadly snakes in the USA. Rattlesnakes usually strike from a coiled position, lunging forward up to two-thirds of their length. They can act very quickly—the Western Diamondback strikes at a speed of 11.5 feet per second.

A Diamondback's rattle

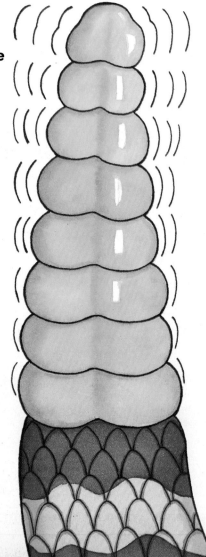

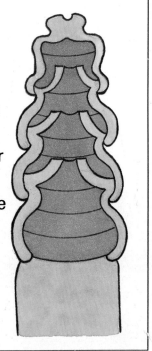

The rattle is made of hollow, loosely linked segments. A new segment is added each time the snake sheds its skin, perhaps four or five times a year. Counting them can give a very rough idea of the snake's age.

Sea snakes

There are many myths and superstitions surrounding sea snakes, the sea serpents of legend. Sailors were supposed to hear the wail of a sea serpent whenever a ship was wrecked.

There are about 50 species of sea snakes living in the warm tropical seas around southern Asia and northern Australia. Their tails are flattened like paddles. Their nostrils are on top of the snout so most of the snake is hidden underwater even when it comes up for air. Many never come out of the water. Only Sea Kraits come ashore to lay their eggs. Others produce live babies at sea. Sea snakes feed mainly on fish. They are highly venomous — one of them has venom a hundred times more potent than that of a land snake.

The fastest swimming sea snake, the Yellow-bellied Sea Snake, can swim at 2.2 mph. Sea snakes can dive down to 330 feet and stay underwater for five hours.

Mythical sea serpent

Snake enemies

Snakes have a number of enemies. They are not even safe from their own kind – the huge King Cobra from Asia feeds almost entirely on other snakes. Birds of prey such as eagles, hawks, owls and Secretary Birds will kill and eat snakes. The little mongoose is one of the best known snake-killers. Usually a mongoose avoids challenging a large cobra, but if there is a fight the mongoose is more likely to win. The snake is no match for the speed, agility and sharp teeth of the mongoose.

Humans are probably the greatest threat to snakes, often killing them unnecessarily, out of fear. People also kill them for their skins, which can be sold for a lot of money.

It takes about eight snakeskins to make a handbag that might cost $150 in the shops.

Secretary Bird trampling a snake

184

Survival file

Although, worldwide, snakebite kills about 30,000 people every year, in most places the risk of death is very small. Even dangerously poisonous snakes often inject little or no poison when biting in self-defense. Most victims are farmers who work barefoot in tropical places where hospitals are hard to reach.

You should always take care when walking in country where snakes live. Don't poke about in places where they like to hide. If someone does get bitten they will probably need to be treated with antivenom.

Demonstration of snake-handling for schoolchildren

The Indian Cobra is found around villages in Southern Asia, so people quite often get bitten. Snake farms "milk" cobras for their venom. Large quantities of venom are needed to prepare the antivenom.

The Black Mamba from Africa tries to flee when approached. If its escape route is blocked it rears up and opens its jaws. Any sudden movement now will make it strike. Victims need antivenom right away.

Puff Adders are common in African countries. They hiss loudly when alarmed. They move slowly and usually stay still when approached. People get bitten when they tread on or near a Puff Adder accidentally.

As one of the few northern European snakes, the European Adder is in need of protection. Its habitat is gradually disappearing and it is often killed needlessly.

Many people in the USA are bitten by Diamondback Rattlesnakes, but only a few die. Some victims are more sensitive to snake venoms than others.

Fangs of a Diamondback Rattlesnake

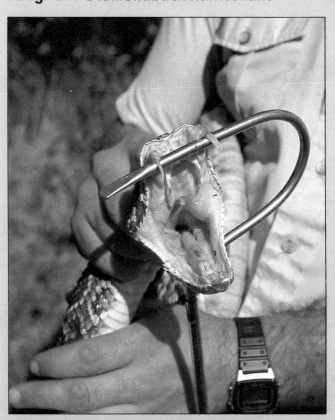

Black Tiger snake being "milked" for venom

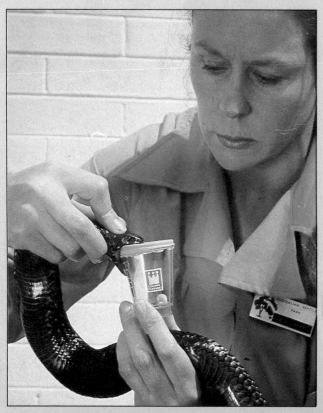

Identification chart

This chart shows you some of the poisonous snakes to look out for in zoos or even in the wild if you are in snake country. They are drawn to scale to show their comparative sizes. The sides of each square on the grid represent 6 inches.

○ N. America
● S. America
○ Europe
○ Africa
○ Asia
○ Australia

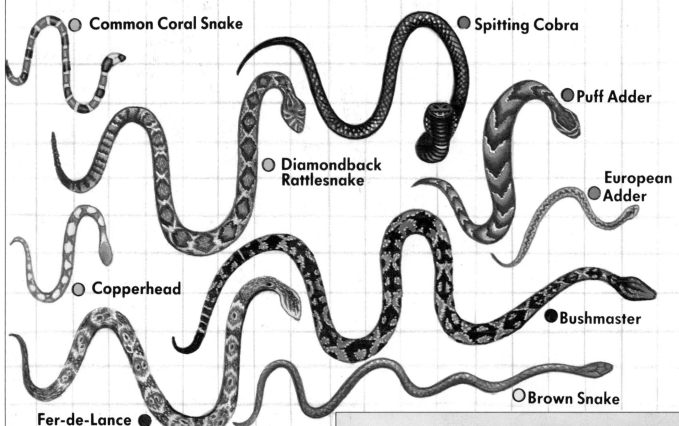

○ Common Coral Snake

○ Spitting Cobra

○ Puff Adder

○ Diamondback Rattlesnake

European ○ Adder

○ Copperhead

● Bushmaster

○ Brown Snake

Fer-de-Lance ●

Make a coiled snake
1. Draw your snake on thin cardboard
2. Color it in, using the chart.
3. Cut around the spiral.
4. Now you have a coiled snake.
5. Balance the snake on a ballpoint pen fixed to a radiator. The warm air will make it turn around.

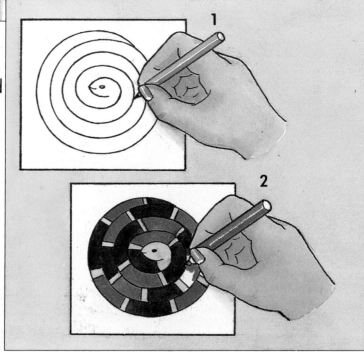

1

2

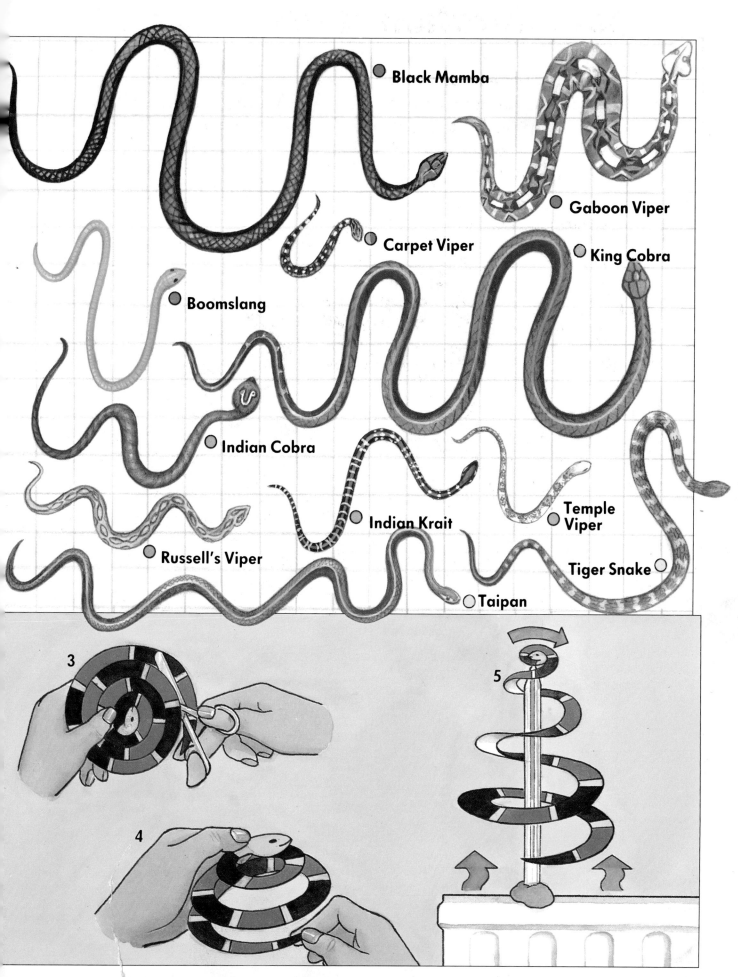

Black Mamba

Gaboon Viper

Carpet Viper

King Cobra

Boomslang

Indian Cobra

Indian Krait

Temple Viper

Russell's Viper

Tiger Snake

Taipan

3

4

5